From Face to Interface: The Shift in Human Connection

Table of Contents

Digital Life and Human Connection **......................................3**

Part 1: The Enduring Power of In-Person Connection **......4**

Chapter 1: Beyond Words: The Multimodality of In-Person Communication **..8**

Chapter 2: A History of Connection: Oral Traditions and Community **..17**

Chapter 3: The Digital Dawn: From Pixels to Networks Worldwide **..25**

Part 2: A Revolutionary Study from Kerala on India's Digital Awakening **..33**

Chapter 4: The Subcontinent Connects: India's Rapid Transition to Digital **..36**

Chapter 5: A Small Example of Change in Rural India: Idukki's Leap **..44**

Chapter 6: Our Journey into the Lives of Students and Teachers: Unpacking the Study **..52**

Part 3: The Digital Student: Managing Identity, Learning, and Relationships **..61**

Chapter 7: My Digital Mirror: My Online Persona, My Personality, and My Identity **..65**

Chapter 8: The Daily Scroll: The Reality of Screen Time, Platforms, and Habits."......73

Chapter 9: The Benefits of Social Media for Academic Success: Learning Outside of the Classroom......82

Chapter 10: The Social Paradox: Are we experiencing less emotion and connecting more?......91

*Chapter 11: The Unspoken Language: When Digital Fails*99

Chapter 12: Academic Headwinds: Burnout, procrastination, and distractions related to technology...107

Part 4: The Teacher's Challenge: Establishing a Connection Between Students of Diverse Ages......116

Chapter 13: The Opinions of an Experienced Teacher: Echoes of the Past......120

Chapter 14: Young Teachers Join the Digital Wave: The New Pedagogy......129

Chapter 15: Navigating the Digital Classroom: Collaborations, Procedures, and Rules......137

Part 5: The Future of Human Connection: Beyond a Screen......153

Chapter 16: The Digital Citizen: Activism, Morality, and Duty on the Internet......157

Chapter 17: The Illusion of Privacy: Our Lives Are Like Open Books......166

Chapter 18: Taking Back Presence: Tips for Living Mindfully in the Digital Age. ***174***

Chapter 19: The Evolving Human: Strategies for Existing in a Hybrid World ***183***

Chapter 20: The Connected Paradox: Combining Our Knowledge and Urging Individuals to Act ***191***

Chapter 21: The Way Forward and the Unanswered Questions ***199***

Conclusion: Strategies for Navigating the Connected Future ***208***

Digital Life and Human Connection

This book conducts an exhaustive investigation of Idukki, Kerala, a distinctive region that is rapidly transitioning to digital technology. It examines one of the most critical enquiries of our era: How is the manner in which we establish interpersonal relationships influenced by our consistent utilisation of social media?

In a society that is increasingly reliant on screens, likes, and instant messaging, the ability to engage in face-to-face communication appears to be waning. However, genuine connections are still established by the warmth of a shared grin, the subtlety of a raised eyebrow, or the comfort of a palm on a shoulder. This book provides a journey to the core of this contemporary paradox, utilising the perspectives and experiences of undergraduate students and professors who are at the forefront of this digital revolution.

This book discusses intriguing facts regarding the impact of social media on our daily lives, learning, and relationships. We will examine the numerous ways in which our digital habits influence us, ranging from the evident advantages of collaborating online and forming new relationships to the less apparent issues of becoming distracted, altering social behaviours, and attempting to be authentic. We should examine the results from Idukki, incorporate some of the more significant global trends, and ultimately determine how we can be more mindful in this interconnected world so that our screens bring us closer to certain individuals without creating a barrier between us and those who are directly in front of us.

Part 1: The Enduring Power of In-Person Connection

In a world that is increasingly digital, where computers are used for a significant portion of our daily interactions, it is easy to believe that the traditional skill of engaging in face-to-face communication is disappearing. However, as this section of our book will demonstrate, the enduring influence of direct human interaction is an indispensable component of our social structure that is indispensable for the establishment of genuine connections, the cultivation of our humanity, and the deepening of our comprehension.

This section establishes the foundation by discussing the significance and distinctiveness of direct human interaction. We commence by deconstructing the "unseen language" that transcends language. Communication is a multimodal symphony that is rich and complex when two individuals meet in person. The meaning is conveyed through a complex choreography of nonverbal clues in addition to spoken language. This encompasses the subtle variations in facial expressions that reveal an individual's true emotions, the numerous messages that body language conveys, the honesty or reluctance in eye contact, and the minor variations in vocal tone. We will discuss the manner in which touch (haptics) and physical distance (proxemics) convey messages without words, as well as the way in which the cadence of a discussion, which includes pauses and response times (chronemics), adds significance that is absent from text-based digital interactions. We will also discuss the neurological foundation of empathy, with a particular emphasis on mirror neurones, which enable us to "feel" and understand the emotions of others when we are in their presence. When we are online, this capability is significantly less advantageous.

It is evident from this comprehensive examination of nonverbal communication that conversing with an individual in person remains crucial for the development of genuine trust and profound empathy. This level of connection and comprehension is difficult to replicate in digital communication due to the ability to read these unspoken signals, witness immediate and unfiltered emotions, and share a physical location. In these direct interactions, we have the opportunity to be open and honest, resolve complex disagreements more effectively, and convey subtle meanings, all of which are crucial for the development of enduring and deep friendships. This section posits that our fundamental requirement for in-person interaction is not merely a social preference, but rather an evolutionary imperative that is inherent in our biology and is crucial for the development of early infancy and the formation of social bonds. For instance, our bodies release neurochemicals such as oxytocin when we interact directly with or touch someone, which further fortifies our social relations.

In order to gain a comprehensive understanding of the current digital transition, we will next consider the manner in which individuals interacted prior to the digital era. We will return to the simpler era, when oral traditions and communal narration were the primary methods of transmitting information, history, and values. Those who read these narratives were able to experience a sense of belonging to a larger and more interconnected entity. We will examine the significance of public spaces such as town squares, markets, and community centres as natural gathering places for individuals to form a sense of community. We will then contrast this with the manner in which individuals frequently engage with one another online, which is more secluded. We will also discuss the ways in which changes such as urbanisation had already begun to affect the manner in which individuals in communities interacted with one another prior to the digital era. These modifications establish the foundation for future modifications.

Finally, this section will provide a concise summary of the history of communication revolutions. It will commence with the telegraph and telephone, which reduced distances while preserving the human voice, and conclude with radio and television, which enabled one-to-many broadcasting and enabled shared cultural experiences without direct interaction. By examining these historical changes, we can observe how the current digital revolution, particularly the emergence of social media, is altering the manner in which we interact with one another in person. The digital world has changed the way we connect inherently due to the fact that mobile connectivity is always on, and social media enables unprecedented many-to-many interaction. This paradox will be thoroughly examined in the subsequent chapters of this book, as it presents both enormous challenges and distinctive opportunities for the enduring power of face-to-face communication.

Chapter 1: Beyond Words: The Multimodality of In-Person Communication

In a world where our lives are reenacted on glowing displays and our thumbs frequently speak more than our mouths, it is effortless to overlook the significance of face-to-face communication, despite the fact that it is the oldest and most fundamental method of human interaction. This is not merely a sterile exchange of words; it is a vibrant symphony of signals, a rich tapestry of expressions, gestures, and an unconscious understanding that transcends language. In order to truly comprehend the numerous ways in which our digital lives are evolving; it is imperative that we first acknowledge the profound and complex nature of direct human interaction.

The Intensity of Nonverbal Cues Beyond Verbal Expressions

Consider a conversation in which only a small portion of the content is truly conveyed, and the emotional impact and complete meaning are beyond the reach of words. This is the complexity of face-to-face communication: it is a dynamic exchange in which meaning is transmitted across numerous channels simultaneously. This attribute, known as multimodality, implies that we are perpetually engaged in a complex interplay of signals that transcends the literal translation of languages. This establishes a comprehensive comprehension that digital communication frequently experiences difficulties in reproducing.

For instance, proxemics and haptics are two forms of communication that employ physical space and contact in a subtle yet effective manner. Whether we intend to or not, the distance we maintain from others reveals a great deal about our connection, level of comfort, and cultural background. In one culture, standing in close proximity may be perceived as confrontational or excessively personal, whereas in another, it may be perceived as a demonstration of affection and interest. A gentle pat on the arm can convey the message "I am here for you," "I care about you," or "I am here for you."

A firm handshake can convey "I trust you" or "I am a professional." These implicit signals of space and contact are a critical component of our communication. They provide us with immediate, visceral feedback that influences our perceptions of the other individual and the relationship. When communicating through screens, these critical components are absent, which may diminish the appeal of our interactions and result in the loss of critical information that our minds are designed to process.

Chronemics, or the implicit language of time in communication, is equally significant. In a face-to-face discourse, the length of pauses, the speed of responses, and the timing of interruptions all have significance. A deliberate delay may indicate that an individual is genuinely contemplating a matter, while a rapid, overlapping response may indicate that they are impatient or eager. The emotional depth and comprehension of a conversation are derived from its flow, the moments in which both individuals remain silent, and the instances in which they both chuckle and gesture simultaneously. This is markedly distinct from digital communication, which is characterised by desynchronised response periods and reliance on external factors rather than immediate interaction. If you fail to respond promptly to a message, individuals may perceive you as uninterested or disrespectful, even if you were simply preoccupied with other tasks. This demonstrates how time signals that are so evident in person can be easily misinterpreted and perplexing when viewed online.

Furthermore, mirror neurones significantly influence our capacity to comprehend and sympathise with others when we engage in direct communication. These remarkable brain cells are activated not only when we perform an action, but also when we observe another individual performing the same action. Our own mirror neurones for smiling activate when we observe an individual smiling, enabling us to intuitively "feel" or comprehend the sensation. Our brains discreetly replicate similar emotions when we observe an individual scowl or make a gesture of anger, enabling us to swiftly and intuitively comprehend the emotions of the other individual. This mirroring mechanism is a critical component of empathy, enabling us to understand and relate to the experiences of others on a profound, almost unconscious level. Video conversations attempt to replicate certain visual cues; however, the efficacy of this empathic mirroring system is contingent upon the complete richness of physical presence, which includes subtle body language, shared space, and real-time energetic exchange. The natural development of empathy, which is crucial for strong human interactions, could be impeded by the limited availability of this intricate neural dance online.

The Primal Need: Our Evolutionary Need to Interact with Others in Person

People's desire to establish interpersonal relationships is not merely a social preference or acquired habit; it is a profoundly ingrained evolutionary imperative that is inherent to our being. For thousands of years, the survival of our species was contingent upon our ability to collaborate, coordinate, and understand one another in the same physical space. In order to plan hunts, warn of hazards, exchange resources, and establish the robust social structures that communities required to survive, early humans were compelled to communicate directly with one another. People were able to learn, adapt, and establish intricate social norms as a result of this persistent, rich feedback cycle. The success of our species is significantly influenced by the presence of face-to-face interaction.

This fundamental requirement for interpersonal interaction is evident in our daily lives, beginning at an early age. Social bonding is strongly rooted in the biological premise of being in close proximity to and engaging with other individuals. Oxytocin, which is occasionally referred to as the "love hormone" or "bonding hormone," is released when individuals engage in physical contact, gaze at one another, or spend time in close proximity. This chemical discharge is crucial for the development of trust, connection, and well-being, which in turn fortifies relationships. These neurochemical reactions provide us with a sense of belonging and connection when we embrace a loved one, laugh with a friend, or simply sit in comfortable silence with someone. Despite the fact that information can still be exchanged, social bonds may not be completely formed due to the absence of physical and sensory components in purely digital interactions. This could result in individuals experiencing emotional depletion, despite the fact that they engage in frequent online communication.

Additionally, children's growth and development during their early years are significantly influenced by face-to-face interaction. The primary method by which infants acquire the ability to communicate, regulate their emotions, and interpret social signals is through direct and reciprocal interactions with their careers. A neonate acquires the ability to interpret the tone of a parent's voice, respond to their smile, and replicate their facial expressions. This constructs the neurological circuits that will enable the infant to comprehend others and experience empathy. These early, profound, and diverse interactions are crucial for the development of the ability to comprehend and respond to the emotions of others, regulate one's own emotions, and establish strong relationships with others. There is concern that the social and emotional development of children in the future may be impacted if they do not learn how to interact with others in a direct and physical manner. This could complicate their ability to navigate the complexities of real-world relationships. The necessity for direct human interaction is not solely a cultural aspiration; it is also a fundamental biological and developmental requirement.

The Distinct Function of Face-to-Face Communication in the Development of Trust and Empathy

It is likely that the most significant and distinctive action we can take in both our personal and professional lives is to engage in face-to-face communication. It is unparalleled in its ability to cultivate profound trust and empathy. Interacting with an individual in person allows us to observe their entire humanity. We can observe the sincerity in their eyes, hear the conviction in their voice, observe the small, unconscious signals that often reveal their feelings or intentions, and experience their true emotional state. This comprehensive perspective enables us to evaluate an individual's dependability, ascertain their motivations, and establish a more profound, authentic connection that is exceedingly difficult, if not impossible, to replicate through alternative methods.

Consider the significance of resolving disputes and engaging in negotiations in person. Whether the conversation is emotionally charged or complex, it is almost always more effective to engage in face-to-face communication. In these circumstances, the capacity to detect subtle cues such as a momentary loss of confidence, a defensive posture, or a diminution of tone provides insight that cannot be achieved through verbal communication. Building rapport, or a sense of mutual comprehension and connection, occurs when individuals are present, exchange nonverbal signals, and have an immediate feedback loop that enables them to clarify matters and de-escalate in real time. In the absence of these uncomplicated indicators, digital conversations may rapidly devolve into misunderstandings, tensions may escalate due to tone misinterpretation, and the human touch necessary to establish lasting agreements and identify common ground may be absent. Being vulnerable and able to respond immediately in person is the most effective method for many individuals to navigate these challenging situations. Additionally, face-to-face settings foster sincerity and vulnerability in direct engagement in a manner that is not facilitated by other settings. We are more inclined to be candid when we are physically present with someone. The immediate reactions of the individual with whom we are conversing are akin to a potent mirror that exacerbates the difficulty of concealing our genuine emotions or maintaining a façade. People may develop a greater sense of trust in one another if they perceive the "real" person without any editing or filtering. In person, it is often more comfortable and natural to discuss profound emotions, share personal anecdotes, or request genuine assistance. This is due to the fact that the presence of a sympathetic listener can be both comforting and validating. This encouragement of authenticity and transparency fortifies and fortifies relationships, which are founded on genuine trust and comprehension between the parties. The study's findings indicate that individuals are frequently more content with their communication and are more inclined to disclose personal information when conversing with someone in person rather than over the phone. This demonstrates the potency and enduring nature of face-to-face communication in the establishment of genuine connections between individuals.

Chapter 2: A History of Connection: Oral Traditions and Community

In order to truly comprehend the extent to which the digital era has revolutionised society, it is necessary to reflect on a period in which individuals engaged in a significantly different manner. Before the advent of displays that were perpetually on, notifications that were perpetually buzzing, and social networks that were both vast and frequently superficial, life and connection were predicated on direct interaction and physical proximity. This chapter prompts us to contemplate the experience of being a part of a society in which communication is a skill that is acquired through everyday interactions. This would offer a unique sense of community and presence that is markedly different from the hyper-connected world we currently inhabit.

The Way We Connected in Less Complex Times: Conversation and Community

Prior to the widespread adoption of digital technology, individuals frequently convened in person, which was a significant aspect of society. Communities were not merely geographic locations; they were vibrant hubs of social interaction that occurred spontaneously and frequently, without any premeditation. The initial "social networks" were the village square, the local market, the common well, or the front porch of a home. Individuals engaged in direct communication and exchanged news, stories, and support.

These kinder eras were characterised by oral traditions and storytelling. Before the majority of individuals were able to read and write, and there was an abundance of printed materials, individuals primarily communicated through discourse to share knowledge, history, morals, and entertainment. The knowledge of elders would be shared, epic stories would be told around fireplaces, and local legends would unite people. This was not merely passive listening; it was a highly interactive process in which individuals collaborated to ascertain the significance of various concepts. The storyteller observed the audience's response and adjusted the narrative to maintain their interest. The performance was further enhanced by the audience's immediate feedback and attendance. This direct, communal act of storytelling not only facilitated intellectual comprehension, but also evoked emotions and provided a shared cultural identity that unified individuals.

Additionally, the organisation and cadence of daily life rendered public spaces even more crucial for human interaction and the development of community. Village squares were not merely locations where individuals passed by; they were also locations where individuals congregated, exchanged greetings, and disseminated local news. Markets were vibrant locations where individuals could engage in conversation, exchange goods, and purchase and sell. News disseminates at the same rate as merchandise. Companions convened at communal wells, washing facilities, or neighbourhood businesses. These locations fostered informal conversations and fortified neighbourhood connections. Even churches and temples, which are places of worship, were significant communal centres where individuals could convene for shared experiences and extended discussions. In an effort to allure individuals to remain, observe, and interact by chance, these physical spaces were designed to establish a perpetual tapestry of direct human interaction that was deeply ingrained in the fabric of life.

It is also crucial to bear in mind that societal changes had already begun to alter community structures prior to the digital era. The impact of urbanisation on traditional communal connections was already a significant transformation. The spontaneous, informal encounters that were prevalent in rural life began to diminish as individuals transitioned from small, tightly connected villages to large, anonymous cities. The evolution of the nuclear family model and the longer commutes that accompany city living make it more difficult to encounter individuals by chance. Cities often lacked the natural, built-in sense of community that smaller, more localised places possessed, despite the fact that they had a broad range of social clubs and professional networks that facilitated connections with others. This historical context serves as a reminder that the challenges associated with conventional face-to-face communication were not initiated by the internet; rather, they exacerbated and evolved in response to its introduction.

The Art of Listening: Communication Before the Internet

The natural development of presence and the highly valued skill of listening were two of the most noticeable distinctions in communication prior to the internet. In the past, individuals were more cognisant of the individual in front of them, as they were not confronted with the multitude of distractions that vie for our attention today. Typically, speakers had the entire attention of their audience when they were not in possession of a smartphone. This enabled all individuals to be heard, rather than only occasionally.

Individuals who engaged in conversation in these circumstances were acutely aware of the significance of silence and pauses. In the past, pauses in speech were typically considered to be significant components of the discourse. However, silence may now be perceived as unwelcoming or as an indication that an individual is not responding. They allowed enough time for presenters to reflect and for the audience to comprehend the content. The discourse could be improved rather than deteriorated by a well-timed delay, which could add emphasis, demonstrate emotional weight, or communicate a change in idea. This gradual tempo prompted individuals to contemplate their words and responses more thoroughly, a stark contrast to the impulsive and rapid manner in which individuals communicate online today.

Additionally, oral civilisations' emphasis on memory and recall fostered the development of distinct cognitive abilities that were associated with memory and attention. Before the majority of individuals were able to read and write, they relied heavily on their memories to recollect and share information, tales, and knowledge. People became more adept at actively listening as a result of the fact that knowledge could not be simply consulted or reread. People devised intricate memory aids and storytelling techniques to facilitate their memory retention, and listening became a more active, deliberate process that necessitated their undivided mental attention. This is in stark contrast to the current digital environment, in which the ubiquitous presence of search engines and external memory devices (such as smartphones) may inadvertently diminish the necessity for prolonged attention to information and profound personal recollection.

A Brief History of Communication Revolutions (and the Unique Characteristics of This One)

Civilisations and the manner in which individuals interact with one another have been significantly altered by numerous communication revolutions that have occurred throughout history. These advancements were substantial, ranging from the development of spoken language, which enabled the collective memory and complex thought processes, to the development of writing, which enabled the transmission and preservation of information across generations and vast distances.

The telegraph and telephone, which were introduced in the 1800s, represented significant advancements. They reduced the perceived distance and preserved the human voice. The telegraph enabled the rapid transmission of text messages over vast distances, thereby expediting the dissemination of news and commerce. The telephone was a truly revolutionary technology that directly introduced the human voice into residences and businesses. It enabled the establishment of real-time connections with individuals across vast distances that were previously considered impractical. Although these technologies enabled communication over vast distances, they lacked the visual cues that are inherent in a face-to-face conversation. Rather, they primarily employed aural (telephone) or textual (telegraph) channels. They were primarily employed for one-on-one communication, which facilitated direct communication between two individuals.

Subsequently, the 20th century witnessed the emergence of radio and television, which initiated one-to-many broadcasting. These forms of mass media enabled millions of individuals to simultaneously access information, entertainment, and cultural narratives. They organised cultural events that were accessible to all, fostering a sense of community around popular performances or national events.

However, these were primarily passive methods of media consumption; audiences were receivers and had minimal, if any, direct interaction with the broadcasters or each other through the medium. Rather than facilitating direct communication, they provided access to a vast array of content and ideas.

The current digital revolution, particularly the increase in social media usage, is distinct from all other communication revolutions in that it enables the establishment of many-to-many connections. Social media platforms differ from broadcast media, which connects one individual to numerous others, and the telephone, which only connects one individual to another. Social media enables individuals to share their opinions, content, and receive responses from a vast, interconnected network of peers, often in real time. Each user is empowered to act as both a creator and a consumer in this interactive, user-generated content, which renders it difficult to distinguish between audience and producer. The constant availability of smartphones and the unprecedented level of interconnectedness have made digital communication an integral part of daily life. It is perpetually present and alters our interactions in ways that face-to-face communication has never been capable of accomplishing.

Chapter 3: The Digital Dawn: From Pixels to Networks Worldwide

The turn of the millennium significantly altered the manner in which individuals communicate, thereby altering the basis of their connections. A small group of computers quickly evolved into a global phenomenon, establishing a new digital environment that has transformed the way we live our daily lives. This chapter discusses the rapid expansion of the internet and the subsequent acceleration of social media. It also discusses the "always-on" mentality that has emerged as a result of the internet.

A Timeline of Digital Progress: The Rise of the Internet

The internet has been in existence for decades in theory, but it truly took off and became a significant component of daily life in the early 2000s, undergoing various phases of evolution.

Web 1.0, the initial phase, was primarily composed of inert websites that functioned as digital brochures or storage locations for information. Consider the initial business homepages, online encyclopaedias, or basic personal webpages. The majority of the time, users were merely perusing content without engaging with it or making any contributions. The internet was typically only accessed and used on desktop computers in specific areas, and connections were occasionally sluggish due to the shrill sounds of dial-up modems. Consequently, it was more difficult to access and use. There was a clear distinction between individuals who created content (webmasters) and those who utilised it.

However, it was not until the mid-2000s that Web 2.0 finally emerged that significant changes began to occur. This was less about altering technology and more about altering the way people thought, empowering them to be active participants, collaborators, and creators. The internet underwent a rapid transformation into a dynamic and captivating environment. Individuals could effortlessly exchange ideas through blogs (such as Blogger and WordPress), collaborate on content through wikis (such as Wikipedia), and, most importantly, establish personal profiles and engage with others on early social networking sites. This paradigm of user-generated content democratised the process of publishing and interacting, transforming the internet from a platform for reading to one that allowed users to write.

The Dot-Com Boom and Bust of the late 1990s and early 2000s were among the most infamous outlandish speculations during this period of tremendous growth. During this period, a significant amount of capital was invested in internet-based businesses, many of which were founded on business concepts that were yet to be proven. The collapse of the bubble resulted in the failure of numerous businesses and the subsequent financial losses. However, it served as a critical early lesson in the pursuit of digital ambition. The recession facilitated the development of more sustainable business models and a greater emphasis on user value. It also constructed the infrastructure and fostered innovation, which would ultimately result in the Web 2.0 eruption. Many of the fundamental concepts and technologies that endured during this period were crucial to the internet's subsequent development.

People were able to remain online at all times due to the ubiquitous use of Wi-Fi and broadband. By eliminating the irritating slowdowns that were characteristic of dial-up, broadband internet simplified online activities. Additionally, it enhanced the speed and reliability of connections. Users no longer had to endure repeated disconnections or wait for a single image to display for minutes. Simultaneously, Wi-Fi technology enabled individuals to connect to the internet without the need for physical wires. This enabled individuals to establish wireless connections in their residences, workplaces, and public spaces. The internet's mobility and pace ensured that it was consistently accessible. This facilitated the integration of online activities into daily life and established the foundation for the mobile-first social media revolution.

In the present day, what is the term "Social Media"? Let us establish our digital playground. In the ever-evolving internet landscape, social media emerged as a revolutionary method of communication and interaction with others, in addition to as a novel type of website. Social media comprises internet-based applications and platforms that enable users to generate and distribute content. The exact features may vary, but they typically enable individuals to establish public or semi-public profiles within a restricted system, compile a list of other users with whom they are connected, and view and navigate their list of connections and those made by others in the system.

The primary characteristics of social media platforms are the defining characteristics of this digital domain. Among these are user profiles, which function as digital identities; friend networks or followers, which facilitate the connection of users; content creation tools, which enable users to post text, photos, videos, and links; and algorithmic feeds, which present content to users based on their prior interactions and preferences. These attributes collectively establish a dynamic environment in which users are not merely passive consumers, but also active participants in a continuous exchange of information and interactivity.

Some of the first social networking sites that paved the way for the major social media platforms of today were Friendster (2002), Myspace (2003), and Orkut (2004), which was particularly popular in Brazil and India. My Space's popularity was attributed to its ability to allow users to customise their profiles in a variety of ways and to establish a robust music and subculture community, while Friendster was primarily focused on connecting individuals who were already acquaintances. Orkut, which was initiated by Google, achieved significant popularity in certain markets due to its emphasis on community development. These websites, which concentrated on personal profiles and buddy networks, were the initial stages towards the development of social media. Nevertheless, they encountered challenges with scalability, design, and competitiveness over time. This facilitated Facebook's ascension to the status of the most widely used social network. It was initiated in 2004 and quickly outperformed its predecessors by providing a superior user experience and a broader audience.

Currently, the digital realm is characterised by a vast array of social media categories, each of which serves a distinct purpose and facilitates interaction. We observe professional networking sites such as LinkedIn, which are dedicated to career advancement; visual sharing sites like Instagram and Pinterest, which are all about aesthetics and photos; short-form video applications like TikTok, which are all about viral, entertainment-driven content; microblogging services like X (formerly Twitter), which are all about the rapid dissemination of news and public conversations; and messaging applications like WhatsApp and Telegram, which have evolved beyond simple text to include voice calls, video calls, group chats, and file sharing, becoming the primary method of communication for billions of individuals. "Social media" is not a singular entity; it is a multifaceted network of technologies that influence the manner in which individuals interact with one another. This is due to the vastness and frequent evolution of the ecosystem.

The "Always-On" Culture Is Now the New Normal

The widespread use of cell phones was the catalyst that truly transformed social media from a computer-based activity to a ubiquitous phenomenon. The manner in which we access the internet was significantly altered by these mobile devices. It became a constant companion, rather than a destination we visited. You could access the internet from any location and at any moment by carrying a smartphone. This initiated a phenomenon that can only be described as the "always-on" culture, in which billions of individuals are accustomed to being online.

The smartphone has made it simpler for everyone to access the internet than it has ever been. You could now access the internet from anywhere, at any time, as it was essentially in the pocket. You were no longer required to possess a computer in order to access the internet. Social media became an integral component of daily life, from commuting to waiting rooms, meals to late nights, as a result of the mobility of individuals. People anticipated prompt responses and consistent updates as a result of this continuous availability, which made it difficult to differentiate between different aspects of life.

This digital bond is further fortified by the psychology of notifications and the necessity of constant connectivity. Social media platforms and applications are meticulously designed to maintain users' interest by employing psychological principles. Notifications, whether they are a visual alert, an audible ping, or a quiet vibration, are intended to stimulate our interest and exploit our "fear of missing out" (FOMO). Each alert is akin to a minor reward, providing an opportunity to acquire new knowledge or gain social acceptance. This compels you to consistently monitor the alerts. This consistent stream of notifications maintains users' interest at all times, rendering it difficult to completely disengage, even when they attempt to concentrate on non-online activities.

The distinctions between work, living, and social life are becoming increasingly muddled as a result of this "always-on" society. The distinction between work time, free time, and time spent with companions has become more challenging to discern. Work communications may be received on a personal phone at the end of the night. Personal conversations may transpire at work, and social media updates may interfere with academic pursuits. This new normal, which provides unparalleled convenience and flexibility, can also be detrimental to mental health, resulting in stress, anxiety, and a sense of being constantly overwhelmed by the demands of a hyper-connected life. It can also make it more difficult to truly disconnect, increase cognitive load, and make you feel like you are always "on call."

Part 2: A Revolutionary Study from Kerala on India's Digital Awakening

After discussing the significance of face-to-face communication, let us examine a real and intriguing case study: India's remarkable digital transformation. This section of the book provides a critical context for our innovative research by examining the manner in which digital change has occurred in the subcontinent and the location of our inquiry.

We commence by discussing the ambitious "Digital India" initiative, a government initiative that was initiated in 2015 with the objective of transforming India into a knowledge economy and digitally empowered society. This section will provide a more comprehensive examination of the various components of the project, including the "Public Internet Access Programme" and "e-Governance," and the methods they employed to bridge the connectivity divide and ensure that digital services are accessible to all. We will also discuss the challenges associated with this extensive undertaking, including the challenges posed by India's numerous languages, infrastructure deficiencies in rural areas, and gaps in digital literacy.

After that, we will examine the rapid expansion of internet and mobile phone usage in the subcontinent, particularly following 2015. During this period, digital adoption experienced an unprecedented surge, largely due to the disruptive emergence of companies such as Reliance Jio, whose ultra-cheap data plans revolutionised the way people access the internet. We will discuss the rapid expansion of low-cost smartphones, which has democratised access to digital devices for millions of individuals. Additionally, we will examine how this development has altered the traditional digital divide between rural and urban areas. We will also examine the distinctive landscape of Indian social media, examining the development of regional language content and homegrown platforms in addition to the significant impact of Indian pop culture and events on internet usage. This will extend beyond the major global players.

The narrative then transitions to Idukki, a picturesque region in Kerala, and elucidates the reasons why it was the ideal location for this thorough dive. We will discuss the distinctive mountainous environment, the predominantly agricultural economy, and the dispersed population of Idukki. Additionally, we will discuss the manner in which the introduction of 4G in 2015 resulted in a minor transformation in rural India. This section will demonstrate the impact of high-speed internet on daily life, including the ability of producers to monitor market prices and individuals to obtain medical advice from afar. Additionally, it will address the social and cultural implications that transcended mere data. Kerala has a high literacy rate, and Idukki was the first district in India to receive comprehensive 4G coverage. This renders Idukki an exceptional "living laboratory" for observing the real-time transformation of society by technology, thereby addressing critical research voids in the adoption of digital technologies in rural areas.

Lastly, this section provides a summary of our research methodology and enumerates the primary enquiries that served as the foundation for our investigation into the impact of social media on in-person communication. The following section will provide a comprehensive explanation of our robust mixed-methods approach and the significance of integrating quantitative surveys with qualitative interviews to obtain a comprehensive understanding. This encompasses a more comprehensive discussion of the methods by which we defined and quantified "face-to-face communication" and "social media use," as well as the primary hypotheses that informed our research. The primary emphasis of this work is on the experiences of undergraduate students and their instructors. Our research is founded on the diverse experiences and perspectives of the individuals in Idukki, which provide the extensive data that substantiates the book's subsequent findings.

Chapter 4: The Subcontinent Connects: India's Rapid Transition to Digital

The digital revolution was underway in the rest of the world when India initiated its own rapid and unique ascent into the interconnected world. The subcontinent has undergone significant transformations since the implementation of a new digital infrastructure and restricted internet access. It is currently one of the most active and expansive online markets in the globe. The digital awakening of India is examined in this chapter, which examines the factors that have contributed to this development, including the vast number of individuals who use mobile phones and ambitious government initiatives. It also examines the distinctive social media environment that has emerged throughout the nation.

The Digital India Vision: Addressing the Connectivity Deficit

The government's "Digital India" initiative, which was initiated in 2015, has played a significant role in the country's digital expansion. The objective of this vast undertaking was to transform India into a digitally enabled society and economy. It encompassed a diverse array of objectives, including the enhancement of the nation's internet infrastructure, the promotion of digital literacy, and the availability of government services online.

The "Digital India" concept was founded upon a number of significant pillars, each of which concentrated on a distinct aspect of the country's digital development. The initiative encompassed more than the construction of "Broadband Highways" to ensure that all individuals could access the internet. It also encompassed a "Public Internet Access Programme" that was designed to establish Wi-Fi nodes and common service centres in rural areas, enabling individuals who did not have their own internet connections to access the internet. One of the primary objectives was "e-Governance: Reforming Government through Technology," which sought to digitise government services in order to enhance their efficiency, transparency, and usability for citizens online, while simultaneously reducing corruption and red tape. The objective of "e-Kranti (Electronic Delivery of Services)" was to ensure that a diverse array of public services, such as health and education, were accessible online. Furthermore,

"Information for All" endeavoured to facilitate the discovery of government data and information for all individuals. "Electronics Manufacturing" was encouraged to assist India in the development of digital products, thereby bolstering its own capabilities. Lastly, the "Early Harvest Programmes" and "IT for Jobs" initiatives were designed to provide citizens with immediate digital advantages and expand employment opportunities in the IT sector. The objective of this comprehensive strategy was to provide individuals with more than just internet access. It was intended to establish a robust digital ecosystem that could facilitate a wide range of services, including e-governance, online education, digital commerce, and healthcare.

However, it was inevitable that the implementation of such an ambitious initiative in a country as vast and diverse as India would be challenging. The significant challenge was the mere magnitude of the infrastructure development required to connect remote and difficult-to-reach areas. This frequently necessitated devising innovative methods to install fibre optic cables or construct mobile antennae. These disparities in digital literacy were also a significant issue. Many individuals, particularly those who resided in rural areas or were elderly, lacked the fundamental skills necessary to effectively utilise the internet, even when they had access.

Additionally, the vast number of languages spoken in India necessitated the provision of digital information and interfaces in more than one regional language, which posed a significant challenge in terms of design and localisation. Regardless of any challenges, the strategic initiative of Digital India laid a foundation that facilitated the rapid adoption of digital technologies, such as social media, by individuals in regions that had previously lacked high-speed internet.

After 2015, there was an increase in the number of individuals who were using the internet and mobile phones. India experienced an unprecedented surge in the utilisation of mobile phones and the internet following 2015. This resulted in a rapid transformation of the nation's digital environment. This increase was the result of a convergence of technological advancements and robust market forces.

One of the most significant and disruptive factors in this rise was the "Jio Effect," which commenced in late 2016 with the entry of Reliance Jio into the telecommunications industry. Jio's ambitious strategy entailed the provision of free voice calls for life and a highly affordable, rapid 4G broadband service, thereby increasing the accessibility of the internet to all. In an effort to preserve their ability to compete, existing telecommunications companies were required to significantly reduce their own data expenses. As a result, the cost of mobile internet decreased significantly across the nation. In the span of a few years, India transitioned from having data that was relatively expensive to having some of the lowest mobile broadband pricing in the world. This decrease in cost rendered the internet no longer a luxury, but rather a practical service that was accessible to a greater number of individuals, particularly those with lower incomes who were previously unable to afford it. Jio's rapid expansion of subscribers, which reached hundreds of millions in record time, revolutionised the telecommunications industry and enabled millions of individuals to access the internet for the first time.

Simultaneously, the proliferation of inexpensive handsets was a significant factor in the emergence of the mobile internet. Android devices that are affordable are frequently sold at reduced prices by both domestic and international companies, thereby enabling millions of Indians to access digital devices. These handsets and the new, inexpensive data plans became the primary method of accessing the internet for a significant number of new users, particularly those residing in rural or semi-urban areas. Their pre-installed programs and user-friendly interfaces made it effortless for individuals who had never used them before to access the internet, utilise social media, and view digital content without the need for a computer.

This combination of inexpensive data and simple-to-locate devices significantly impacts the digital divide between rural and urban areas. In the past, the majority of urban residents had access to digital infrastructure and the internet, while the majority of rural residents did not.

Nevertheless, the rapid deployment of 4G networks, which was facilitated by government initiatives and competition, was specifically designed to establish connectivity in rural areas. The gap between these two categories has been significantly reduced since 2015. However, there may still be some discrepancies in access to advanced digital services or consistent quality. High-speed internet is now accessible to millions of individuals in rural India. This enables them to engage with the global community in previously unimaginable ways, obtain an education online, and participate in the digital economy. At present, India is the world's second-largest internet market, following China. The foundation for the significant changes in society that are currently occurring was established by the accelerated growth of the online population.

The Indian Social Media Scene: Beyond Global Giants

Facebook and WhatsApp are the most widely used social media platforms worldwide; however, India is a dynamic and distinctive environment in which these titans coexist and are frequently influenced by local differences and emerging platforms.

The vast number of languages spoken in India has resulted in a significant demand for materials and platforms in regional languages. Facebook and Google, global corporations, implemented modifications by incorporating interfaces and content in numerous Indian languages, including Bengali, Malayalam, Tamil, and Hindi. This also facilitated the development of Indian applications that could satisfy this cultural and linguistic requirement. In general, individuals prefer to read and write in their native languages, which fosters a vibrant community of content creators and consumers who are proficient in those languages. The emphasis on indigenous languages has been a significant factor in the differentiation of Indian social media from that of other countries. It has engaged individuals who reside in urban areas and do not speak English. Social media trends and the manner in which individuals utilise it throughout the nation are also significantly influenced by Indian contemporary culture and events. Major cultural events, such as the Indian Premier League (IPL) and the highly regarded Twenty20 cricket league, garner significant online attention. The activities are followed by millions of followers, who discuss them in real time and share content on platforms such as Facebook and X (formerly Twitter). The vibrant Bollywood and regional film industries, which include Malayalam, Tamil, and Telugu cinema, also generate a significant amount of social media conversation regarding new films, celebrity news, and fan groups. Additionally, significant holidays such as Diwali, Holi, and Eid serve as platforms for individuals to exchange greetings, post content, and commemorate the occasion online. This demonstrates the extent to which India's culture is interconnected with social media.

This unique industry has also resulted in the expansion of Indian-made applications, which have amassed substantial user bases by identifying and satisfying the requirements of local users. Two examples of this trend are ShareChat, a social media application that concentrates on regional languages, and Moj, a short-video platform that gained popularity, particularly after certain foreign applications were prohibited as a result of geopolitical events. These applications, which are developed in India, frequently emphasise content that is popular among Indian users, accommodate cultural distinctions, and facilitate the creation of content in the user's native language. The success of these platforms demonstrates that, despite the presence of numerous large global corporations in India, the country's social media landscape is evolving due to the fact that they are able to effectively accommodate to the diverse languages and cultures of the subcontinent.

Chapter 5: A Small Example of Change in Rural India: Idukki's Leap

There was a substantial digital transition in India as a whole, but certain regions were at the forefront of this change, providing us with valuable insights into the practical effects of connectivity. Among these, Idukki is one of Kerala's most attractive and distinctive districts. It is the ideal location for our comprehensive investigation due to its transition to the high-speed internet era, which serves as a prime illustration of the impact of digital advancements on a predominantly rural populace.

The 4G Revolution: The Impact of High-Speed Internet on a District

Idukki achieved a significant milestone in 2015 as part of the ambitious Digital India initiative: it became the first district in India to have comprehensive 4G internet service. This was not merely a minor technological advancement; it was a significant transformation that enabled individuals in a region with a unique social and economic structure and challenging terrain to communicate in a manner that had never been possible before.

This transition was rendered even more significant by the unique topography and population of Idukki. Kerala's second-largest district is Idukki. The majority of the area is rural, and a significant portion is comprised of dense forests, undulating mountains, and numerous plantations. Tea, coffee, cardamom, and rubber comprise the primary commodities, which are the foundation of the economy. The inhabitants reside in valleys and slopes. Many of these remote locations were either without internet access, had to rely on faulty dial-up connections, or were too costly to access it prior to 2015. Many individuals believed that high-speed internet would never be feasible due to the difficulty of installing fibre optic connections across mountains. Therefore, the introduction of 4G was not only a technological advancement, but also a lifeline that connected cities that had been isolated from the global digital network to the rest of the world.

The district's daily life was significantly impacted by the 4G revolution in a variety of ways that were dispersed. For instance, farmers who previously depended on word of mouth or a limited number of market visits could now immediately access real-time market pricing for their crops. This enabled them to make more informed decisions and potentially generate higher returns. Local artists who excelled in traditional crafts discovered novel revenue streams by utilising social media to showcase their work to a broader audience than just local tourism. They may also be able to sell their work online and reach customers in other countries. Remote consultations were enabled in the healthcare sector, facilitating communication between individuals in rural communities and physicians in urban areas through the use of technology. This reduced the necessity for lengthy journeys to obtain fundamental medical guidance. Students were the primary focus of our investigation, as they were able to immediately access educational resources, online tutorials, and collaborative learning platforms. This significantly altered their learning process. The profound impact of the digital revolution on the daily lives of individuals in Idukki was demonstrated by these tangible changes.

However, the transition to 4G was not without its challenges, and numerous complications were encountered during the transition. Despite the installation of the infrastructure, numerous residents, particularly the elderly, required assistance in utilising the new connectivity due to their lack of familiarity with the system. Another issue was that individuals were averse to change due to their accustomed approach to tasks. Additionally, the network's stability and the reliability of services were impeded by the difficulty of maintaining a robust infrastructure in the rugged terrain of Idukki, which is susceptible to heavy monsoons and landslides. These issues demonstrated that, despite the rapid implementation of technology, the individuals and environment that influence its use and long-term consequences are equally significant.
The social and cultural implications of connectivity in Idukki extend beyond data.
The transformations in Idukki went beyond mere improvements in internet speed and technology accessibility; they also initiated a genuine transformation in the manner in which individuals interacted with one another and lived in the

community. 4G internet is now accessible and reasonably priced, which has resulted in a rapid shift in the behaviour of individuals, particularly students. This resulted in both anticipated advantages and unforeseen complications. The economy and local enterprises were the most severely affected. Digital payment systems enabled small store proprietors to reduce their dependence on cash and expand their customer base. Small internet enterprises may be established by homemakers, who use social media groups to sell their handmade crafts or products. This would result in a new era of micro-entrepreneurship. Larger agricultural enterprises were capable of more effectively managing their supply chains due to their ability to establish connections with a greater number of individuals. This allowed them to more easily plan their logistics. Although the digital infrastructure did not entirely alter the situation, it did introduce a new level of efficiency and potential that facilitated the expansion of the local economy.

Additionally, 4G significantly altered the manner in which families communicated, particularly those with relatives who reside in different regions of India or labour abroad. Kerala has a significant number of expatriates, and in the past, communication with family members was limited to costly phone calls or letters, which were not frequent occurrences. Video conversations became a common occurrence as a result of the widespread availability of high-speed internet, enabling families to communicate and interact in real time. This resulted in a greater sense of emotional intimacy and connection following their relocation. This continuous visual and auditory connection facilitated the preservation of familial and cultural connections, thereby mitigating some of the social expenses associated with relocation for employment.

Community involvement and the dissemination of information were significantly impacted on a broader scale. People have the ability to exchange and receive information regarding local news, neighbourhood events, and government programs at an unprecedented tempo. WhatsApp groups emerged as the primary venue for neighbourhood associations, religious groups, and local organisations to convene, facilitating the rapid exchange of information and the development of plans. During local emergencies or communal projects, information could be disseminated rapidly, facilitating the collaboration of individuals at a much quicker pace than is customary. This enhanced connectivity resulted in a more informed and potentially more engaged populace, which altered the functioning of local government and the manner in which individuals engaged with society.

The Reason for the Development of This Region as Our Primary Research Facility

We intentionally selected Idukki as the location for our research for strategic reasons, in order to gain a more comprehensive comprehension of the impact of social media on interpersonal communication. The district's unique combination of characteristics rendered it the optimal "living laboratory" for our investigation.

The concept of a "living laboratory" was the most significant factor in our decision. Idukki is the second-largest district in Kerala; however, it is characterised by a significant amount of rural land and a plethora of forests and mountains. This demographic profile enabled us to examine the repercussions of high-speed internet in a rural environment, a perspective that is not frequently encountered in global research. The majority of research on social networking sites concentrates on urban areas, which results in a significant gap in our comprehension of the impact they have on rural areas that are still in the process of development. Idukki was a location that allowed us to observe the evolution of society as high-speed internet became more prevalent.

Secondly, our research was intended to address the voids in our understanding of the adoption of digital technology in rural areas. The relationship between the use of social networking sites and face-to-face communication in a rural district that was also quite digitally sophisticated was not extensively examined in the vast body of research on digital transformation in cities in India. Idukki was the first district in India to achieve complete 4G broadband coverage, which rendered it the ideal location to address this lacuna. In this manner, we could observe the immediate and long-term consequences of a significant technological advancement in a limited, well-defined region.

Finally, the high literacy rate in Kerala is a significant factor in the widespread use of technology. Kerala has consistently maintained the greatest literacy rate in India, and nearly all residents possess a mobile phone. The inhabitants of Idukki were inherently more receptive to and capable of utilising new technologies due to their extensive education. The district is an even more intriguing case study due to the likely influence of this social and educational environment on the speed and manner of 4G adoption in Idukki. The data collection process was facilitated by the consistent and dependable internet connections in Idukki. This meant that connectivity was not a confusable factor, allowing us to concentrate on the behavioural and communication changes that accompanied the widespread use of social media. This unique combination of factors rendered Idukki the ideal and indispensable location for our investigation into the intricate methods by which individuals communicate in the contemporary era.

Chapter 6: Our Journey into the Lives of Students and Teachers: Unpacking the Study

After discussing the significance of face-to-face communication and the distinctive transformation of Idukki as a result of technology, we can now proceed to the primary focus of this book: the meticulous investigation that serves as its underpinning. This chapter provides a comprehensive review of our research, encompassing the specific questions we aimed to address, the meticulous methods we employed, and the individuals—students and teachers in Idukki—whose experiences and perspectives illuminate the intricate relationship between our digital and real-world interactions.

The Primary Question: What is the impact of social media on in-person communication?

One of the primary objectives of our research was to determine the various ways in which social media influences the face-to-face communication between undergraduate students and their lecturers in Idukki. We aimed to transcend personal narratives and employ authentic evidence to elucidate a phenomenon that has a profound impact on nearly every aspect of contemporary life.

Our primary objective was to determine the precise relationship between the use of social media and in-person communication. In order to accomplish this, we meticulously identified and quantified the most critical variables. Implementing "social media usage" necessitated consideration of numerous variables. We enquired about the number of hours that participants spend online each day, with a particular emphasis on the amount of time they spend on social media platforms. Additionally, we enquired about the frequency with which individuals reviewed their social media notifications and feeds (e.g., once an hour or multiple times daily) and the number of distinct social media platforms they utilised on a regular basis. We also examined the amount of money they spent on internet services each month as an indirect measure of their engagement with and access to digital content. Our multifaceted approach enabled us to obtain a comprehensive representation of their digital immersion.

Similarly, the implementation of "face-to-face communication" necessitated a significant amount of consideration. This information was obtained by enquiring with participants regarding the frequency of in-person meetings with their friends, family, and instructors. Additionally, we enquired about the quality of their in-person interactions, such as their level of comfort, the depth of the conversations, and their ability to articulate their thoughts. Enquiries were posed regarding whether they believed that conversing with an individual in person was more meaningful than conversing with them online. As we employed both methodologies, we were able to analyse both the quantitative (frequency) and qualitative (quality) aspects of their direct interactions.

Our investigation was guided by a few primary concepts that were derived from our initial observations and existing knowledge. We believed that there would be a strong correlation between the use of social media and in-person communication; however, we were uncertain as to whether this would be beneficial or detrimental. We also believed that the impact of social media on individuals would vary significantly based on factors such as their gender, academic background (Arts, Commerce, Science), and location (urban versus rural). We also anticipated that instructors, particularly those with more experience, would be concerned about the impact of social media on students' academic performance and communication skills. These concepts facilitated the collection and analysis of our data.

Using a Mixed-Methods Approach in Idukki: Our Research Plan

In order to address these challenging enquiries, our investigation implemented an effective mixed-methods approach that integrated both quantitative and qualitative research methodologies. This dual strategy was not arbitrary; it was predicated on a compelling rationale for employing blended methodologies. We were able to identify generalisable insights by employing surveys to capture quantitative data that demonstrated broad trends, measured relationships, and statistically tested hypotheses across a broad sample. However, numerical data alone cannot demonstrate the depth of human experience or the reasons behind individuals' actions in a more complex manner. We employed in-depth interviews to acquire qualitative data that provided us with the necessary context to examine the thoughts, emotions, worries, and motives of participants in their own words. This enhanced the statistical findings by providing additional depth and significance. Utilising three distinct data sources, we were capable of acquiring a more comprehensive and in-depth understanding of the phenomenon under investigation.

The questionnaire's pilot testing and design were executed with meticulous attention to detail. The author developed a 32-question questionnaire following a comprehensive examination of the existing research on academic achievement, communication patterns, and social media use. It included demographic questions (age, gender, academic discipline, location), 5-point Likert scale items to assess attitudes and perceptions (e.g., "Does social media influence my face-to-face communication in a positive or negative manner"), and open-ended questions to encourage students to provide qualitative responses. The questionnaire was thoroughly tested by a small group of students who were not part of the primary sample prior to its full deployment. During this pilot phase, the tool was developed to ensure its legitimacy and reliability, and any ambiguous terminology was identified. Additionally, the instructions were evaluated for clarity. This necessitated minor modifications to the language in order to facilitate comprehension. Teachers were provided with a semi-structured interview guide for the qualitative component. This enabled a session that was both flexible and guided, ensuring that critical topics were addressed while also allowing interviewees to delve deeper into unexpected revelations. In the interviews, they were asked to discuss their observations of the ways in which students use social media, the impact it has on their academic performance, the manner in which students communicate with one another (both in person and online), and their opinions on the advantages and disadvantages of social media in general. Subsequently, thematic analysis was implemented to evaluate the qualitative data obtained from the interviews. This involved a meticulous review of the interview transcripts, the identification of common themes and concepts, the classification of the transcripts, and the subsequent organisation of the transcripts into larger groups to illustrate the primary stories and perspectives that the instructors expressed.

We employed convenient sampling to select both students and instructors to participate in our investigation. 500 undergraduates were selected from five institutions in the Idukki district due to their strategic locations. A single institution was selected from each of the five taluks (sub-districts) of Idukki. This ensured that both aided and unassisted colleges were represented and that there was a geographical dispersion. It was effortless to recruit 100 students from each institution, and they endeavoured to maintain an evenly distributed number of students in each stream (Arts, Commerce, and Science) to ensure that students from a variety of academic backgrounds were represented. Twenty-five individuals were randomly selected from the same five colleges to serve as educators. Convenient sampling is a non-probability strategy that was selected for practical reasons due to the necessity of conducting the study in a specific geographical area where a sufficient number of individuals could be contacted.

Introducing the Participants: The Inquiry Centres on Students and Teachers

The undergraduate students and their instructors in Idukki were the individuals whose daily lives were most promptly impacted by the digital revolution. This was the focal point of our investigation. The primary data that enabled our comprehensive study were the experiences, thoughts, and actions of the participants.

According to the demographic data of our student participants, they were a representative yet diverse group. The majority of the 500 undergraduate students were young adults, with the majority falling within the age range of 18 to

22, which is a critical period for the development of social skills and identity. The gender distribution was highly uniform, which is indicative of the student body at the colleges. The results were representative of the district's diverse academic environments, as they were distributed nearly evenly among the Arts, Commerce, and Science streams. Idukki is a distinctive location due to its combination of digital sophistication and rurality, as evidenced by the fact that approximately 84.4% of our student participants were from rural areas. Their responses illustrated the manner in which they employ the internet on a daily basis. The internet is an integral part of their lives, as evidenced by the fact that a substantial number of them spend between 2 and 5 hours online each day, and a significant number spend more than 5 hours online. Additionally, their monthly internet service invoices provided us with an understanding of the affordability and simplicity of establishing an internet connection in the region.

The teachers' profiles and experience levels were quite beneficial for comparison. We divided the 25 teachers who provided us with their valuable perspectives through qualitative interviews into two categories: "experienced teachers" and "freshers." "Experienced teachers" were those who had been teaching for one to five years and had begun their careers after 2015, which coincided with the 4G revolution in Idukki. These professors were typically younger and more at ease with technology due to their increased familiarity with it. "Experienced teachers" were individuals who had been teaching for more than five years, and in many cases, for much longer, and had begun their careers prior to 2015. They discussed the manner in which pupils interacted and communicated prior to the widespread availability of high-speed internet. They provided students with a comprehensive understanding of academic life by instructing them in a diverse array of subjects.

The procedures for recruiting participants and obtaining their consent adhered to ethical standards. The principals of the selected colleges provided their official consent prior to the data collection. Teachers were approached individually, while pupils were approached in their classrooms or common areas. Participants were provided with a comprehensive explanation of the study's objectives, the option to participate, and assurances that their identities would remain confidential. All participants who completed the questionnaires or conducted interviews endorsed a document indicating that they comprehended the nature of their duties. This meticulous approach guaranteed that the data we obtained was not only representative and accurate, but also ethical, safeguarding the privacy and well-being of all participants in our investigation.

Part 3: The Digital Student: Managing Identity, Learning, and Relationships

Undergraduate students are not merely passive observers of the digital age; they are its most active inhabitants, engaging in the process of shaping and being influenced by nearly every aspect of it. This critical section of our book provides a comprehensive examination of the lives of these young individuals, allowing us to observe their interactions with the digital world in a variety of ways. It is significantly influenced by the profound insights we acquired during our research in Idukki. In this "Student's Digital Universe," we discover the profound impact of social media on their education, social interactions, and self-perception.

We commence by examining the intricate process of constructing an online persona, in which social media platforms function as digital mirrors that display meticulously selected representations of the self. This entails an understanding of the perpetual pressure that children experience to demonstrate a flawless existence, which is frequently exacerbated by the widespread use of filters and editing tools that establish unattainable beauty standards. We will discuss the "highlight reel" phenomenon, which presents only positive aspects of a story, thereby creating a distorted perception of reality for both the author and the audience. This continuous performance is motivated by the psychological need for validation, which is fuelled by dopamine loops that induce individuals to desire "likes" on social media platforms. This renders the pursuit of "likes" a potent form of social currency. We will also examine the significant influence that digital opinion leaders, or "influencers," have on students' aims and perceptions, as well as the subtle ways in which their commercialised content influences these factors. This prompts ethical enquiries regarding transparency and honesty. This section also discusses the detrimental effects of comparison culture. It elucidates how the internet exacerbates social comparison theory, which can lead to feelings of inadequacy, the "Fear of Missing Out" (FOMO), and impacts on mental health and body image. Doubts about real life frequently arise from online experiences.

The subsequent section of the voyage pertains to the tangible consequences of their consistent social media usage. We will provide a comprehensive analysis of the manner in which students allocate their screen time among various activities, including texting, viewing content, creating content, and playing games, using the quantitative data we have collected from Idukki. We will identify the times and circumstances during which individuals utilise social media the most, demonstrating its integration into every aspect of their day, from commuting to preparing for bed. This research will also investigate the psychological "habit loop" of trigger, routine, and reward that motivates individuals to engage in compulsive social media use. We will examine the evolving landscape of platforms that extend beyond the well-known ones, such as WhatsApp and Facebook. We will concentrate on the rapid expansion of TikTok and Instagram, as well as the allure of short-lived content formats such as "Stories" and "Reels." Additionally, we will discuss the influence of algorithms on content personalisation and the emergence of niche platforms and communities that enable students to connect with others who share their interests. This section is crucial because it addresses the issue of regulating screen time in the "always-on" generation. It examines the impact of constant connectivity on sleep and overall health, as well as the strategies that students frequently attempt but fail to implement in order to regulate their own conduct.

Finally, this section examines the potential for social media to serve as both a beneficial academic resource and a source of issues. We will examine the ways in which it facilitates the collaboration of students in the classroom, such as the use of group discussions, shared notes, and online conversations. Additionally, we will discuss the precise tools and features that enable this. We will also examine the ease with which social media facilitates the connection between teachers and students, as well as the perceptions of students regarding their instructors increased online accessibility. This section also directly addresses the "social paradox" by providing our study findings on the correlation between the use of social media and in-person communication. It also discusses the nuances of this positive relationship, its constraints, and the implications for the social development of students. We will also discuss the "academic headwinds" of digital burnout, procrastination, and distractions, which will demonstrate how notifications can rob the focus and disprove the notion that you can multitask. We will discuss the results of our study, which pertain to the correlation between academic success and the use of social media. This will encompass an examination of the "spelling crisis," which is a phenomenon in which auto-correction impacts fundamental literacy, as well as anecdotes from educators regarding the ways in which students delay their assignments. In addition, we will discuss the implications of this for research skills in general. This comprehensive perspective illustrates the numerous methods by which children engage with their digital environment.

Chapter 7: My Digital Mirror: My Online Persona, My Personality, and My Identity

Our digital identities on social media are not merely internet addresses; they are intricate mirrors that present the world with carefully selected representations of ourselves. These platforms are particularly advantageous for undergraduate students, as they provide them with an opportunity to showcase their desired image, experiment with new identities, and express themselves. This chapter delves into the fascinating and occasionally perplexing realm of the online persona. It examines the stress associated with the pursuit of the ideal digital self, the pervasive influence of digital opinion leaders, and the subtle manner in which comparison culture can influence our most profound offline uncertainties.

The Importance of Demonstrating a Perfect Life: The Creation of the Digital Self

A student initiates a process of self-construction that is often unconscious but extremely significant when they establish a social media presence. Every photo they select, every caption they compose, every filtered image they share, and every update they post contributes to the narrative of their online identity. It is not enough to simply share life experiences; it is also important to establish an online identity that aligns with the objectives, seeks approval, and adheres to social norms. The pursuit of "likes," favourable comments, and follower counts becomes a potent form of social currency, exerting a constant but discreet pressure on individuals to demonstrate a life that is not only pleasant, but also flawless.

This idealised manner of presenting oneself is significantly influenced by filters and editing tools. Photo editing applications and filters that are integrated with social media platforms enable users to meticulously modify their appearance, enhance illumination, smooth their skin, and even alter the contour of their facial features. These tools can assist in the creation of an image that appears flawless; however, they frequently establish beauty standards that are unattainable in real life. Consistently viewing flawless photographs of oneself and others may alter one's perceptions of what constitutes beauty and normalcy. This can cause you to feel dissatisfied with the natural appearance and drive you to strive for perfection at all times. Individuals are under the impression that they are obligated to present a flawless version of themselves, which exacerbates the disparity between their online persona and their authentic self. This issue is further exacerbated by the "highlight reel" obsession. Social media platforms are designed to encourage individuals to showcase only the positive, thrilling, and enviable aspects of their lives. Individuals share photographs of their most thrilling adventures, their academic accomplishments, their seemingly perfect relationships, and their luxurious travels. The daily problems, the dull, the hard, and the unsecure are still significantly absent. This can result in a distorted perception of reality, in which the lives of others appear to be consistently delightful and joyful. The frequent exposure to a carefully selected stream of achievements and happiness can lead students to feel inadequate and isolated, as they contrast their own chaotic, flawed lives with the polished, idealised versions they observe online.

This perpetual pursuit of digital perfection is fuelled by the robust psychological processes of dopamine cycling and affirmation seeking. Dopamine, a chemical associated with reward and satisfaction, is produced by the brain when an individual publishes an item and receives "likes," favourable comments, or new followers. This results in a robust positive feedback loop that motivates individuals to publish and seek approval. The brain releases dopamine each time you receive notification of a new like or comment, which in turn increases the desire for more. Social media may be employed by individuals to secure acceptance from others, rather than to truly convey themselves or prioritise their well-being. This enduring desire for external validation can serve as a significant motivator for utilising social media. This persistent compulsion to perform and pursue digital approbation can have a significant impact on mental health, resulting in anxiety, a sense of being unauthentic, and a diminished sense of self-worth that is determined by the perceptions of others rather than one's own internal experiences.

The Impact of Influencers: Shifting Objectives and Perspectives

New forms of digital opinion leaders have emerged in the contemporary digital landscape, known as influencers. These individuals, who are frequently ordinary individuals who have amassed substantial audiences through their content, possess significant influence over their audience's preferences, opinions, and purchasing decisions. Influencers generate content that is meticulously crafted and pertains to fashion, fitness, travel, gaming, or lifestyle. This gives the impression that they lead a lifestyle that is desirable to young people.

There are two primary categories of influencers: macro-influencers and micro-influencers. Each has a distinct impact. Macro-influencers are frequently renowned and have millions of followers. They possess a significant amount of influence. Their impact is typically extensive, influencing the behaviour of individuals and the direction of trends on a grand scale. Conversely, micro-influencers possess lesser but highly engaged and niche followings. Their impact is generally more pronounced in specific demographics due to the fact that they are perceived as more authentic, relatable, and trustworthy authorities in their respective fields. Influencers of both kinds can serve as contemporary role models for students, subtly influencing their worldview and aspirations by dictating trends in a variety of areas, including clothing, beauty standards, career paths, and travel destinations.

However, this power is perpetually associated with the commercial aspect of power. The distinction between genuine advice and paid advertising is often difficult to discern, as a significant number of influencer postings are either explicitly or subtly commercial. Influencers' earnings are currently primarily generated through brand collaborations, sponsored content, and affiliate marketing. Consequently, their recommendations are frequently financially motivated. This lack of transparency may lead followers to believe that product endorsements are genuine personal recommendations rather than paid marketing. The constant observation of apparently flawless lifestyles, which are often endorsed by brand partnerships and meticulously selected to be as appealing as possible, can establish unrealistic expectations for wealth, success, and happiness, particularly for students who may not fully comprehend the business rationale behind them.

This commercialisation also raises significant moral concerns in the context of influencer marketing. Transparency is of paramount importance, and there are ongoing debates regarding the extent to which influencers disclose sponsored content. In addition, there are concerns regarding authenticity, as the necessity to maintain a positive public image may result in individuals becoming less authentic and more preoccupied with their appearances. Additionally, there is a potential for exploitation, particularly among younger individuals who may be more susceptible to seductive advertising and inaccurate representations of reality. Students are consistently inundated with aspirational content, which is frequently associated with consumption. This can inadvertently advance their objectives in a manner that may not be consistent with their identity, achievable objectives, or long-term health. This fosters a culture of perpetual discontent and yearning.

We are living in a culture of comparison when our online lives cause us to question our actual lives. One of the most prevalent and detrimental aspects of our digital mirror is its persistent encouragement of us to evaluate ourselves in relation to others. Social media platforms are intentionally designed to encourage individuals to compare themselves to others. They provide an infinite number of opportunities to accomplish this. It is common for individuals to compare themselves to others; however, the digital world facilitates this behaviour on a continuous basis, and in circumstances that are occasionally exceedingly unrealistic.

This phenomenon is predicated on the concept of social comparison in the digital era. It is human nature to compare oneself to others. Social media platforms provide an endless stream of "upward comparisons," which are images of individuals who appear to be performing better, having more fun, or accomplishing more. This endless torrent of flawless lives, meticulously curated and presented as flawless, can induce feelings of inferiority, envy, and dissatisfaction with one's own existence. The scope of digital comparison extends beyond a limited circle of friends to encompass hundreds or thousands of "friends" and strangers, which may induce feelings of inferiority.

This culture of comparison is the direct cause of the pervasive Fear of Missing Out (FOMO) and its consequences. Consistently witnessing the enjoyable activities, social gatherings, or excursions of others can induce feelings of anxiety and inferiority. Students may experience feelings of isolation and melancholy when they observe feeds that depict their friends attending parties to which they were not invited or embarking on vacations that they are unable to afford. This persistent sensation that "everyone else is having a better time" can cause individuals to feel compelled to remain connected, monitor updates constantly, and participate in online trends, even if it requires them to sacrifice sleep, study time, or real-life connections. Individuals with FOMO are perpetually in pursuit of an idealised, frequently unrealistic, form of happiness online, which perpetuates a cycle of anxiety and dissatisfaction.

The mental health and body image of individuals are significantly impacted by the constant comparison and anxiety of missing out. The constant exposure to digitally enhanced and frequently unattainable beauty standards promoted by peers and influencers can result in significant body dissatisfaction, particularly among young women. However, this issue is now affecting individuals of all genders. This may manifest as a dietary disorder, excessive exercise, or excessive self-consciousness. In general, the pressure to maintain a flawless online presence and the constant comparisons have been demonstrated to result in elevated levels of anxiety, melancholy, low self-esteem, and even feelings of loneliness, even when one is "connected" to thousands of individuals. The internet is intended to foster connections between individuals; however, it can also induce feelings of isolation and inadequacy in students, as they observe the flawless online lives of others in contrast to the chaotic and defective offline lives they lead. This can result in significant mental health issues and uncertainties.

Chapter 8: The Daily Scroll: The Reality of Screen Time, Platforms, and Habits."

In the digital age, the smartphone has become an almost inseparable component of our identity, and "scrolling" has become a daily habit for all. This daily scroll is not merely a means for college students to pass the time; it is a way of life that influences their learning, social interactions, and mobility in the world. This chapter examines the tangible consequences of students' social media usage. It employs the data from our Idukki study, examines the evolution of popular platforms, and discusses the prevalent challenge of maintaining digital boundaries in a culture that is perpetually connected.

A Day in the Life: The Way in Which Students Utilise Social Media

The research we conducted in Idukki provided us with a comprehensive understanding of the extent to which social media is a prominent aspect of the daily lives of college students. The statistics provided us with a wealth of valuable information regarding their interpersonal interactions, illustrating a generation for whom online communication is an absolute necessity rather than an option. A significant number of the students who participated reported that they dedicated between two and five hours each day to online activities. It is even more surprising that a significant number of students spend more than five hours online each day, demonstrating the significance of digital platforms in their daily activities.

This extended period of time spent in front of a screen is not a single entity; it encompasses numerous other activities. In our investigation, we examined the overall internet usage. However, by examining observations and broader trends, we can make an educated estimate regarding the amount of time individuals allocate to specific activities. A significant portion of this time is devoted to messaging, primarily through applications such as WhatsApp, for both academic and personal group discussions. Content consumption consumes a significant amount of time, including the perusal of image-rich feeds on Instagram, the viewing of videos on YouTube or TikTok, and the reading of news bulletins on multiple platforms. A decreasing but increasing proportion of time is allocated to the creation of content, which may involve students producing and editing brief videos, creating illustrations, or writing blogs. Lastly, a significant number of students devote a significant amount of time to playing games on their smartphones, including both casual and more complex online games. This variety of applications demonstrates the smartphone's versatility, rendering it difficult to distinguish between communication, entertainment, and information acquisition.

Additionally, we determined the most popular times and locations for individuals to utilise social media. The initial time many students utilise their phones is within minutes of waking up, when they check their notifications and updates before moving out of bed. When individuals are strolling or riding a bus, they frequently consult their smartphones. Despite the prohibitions, individuals frequently glance at their social media feeds or messages during lectures. It is not uncommon for individuals to take brief breaks from their studies to inspect their phones, which can result in lengthy perusing sessions. Students frequently utilise social media platforms until the wee hours of the morning. These prevalent usage patterns demonstrate that social media is not merely a hobby; it is a crucial aspect of their daily routine that consumes time during transitions, downtime, and even periods when they would typically be working or resting.

The habit loop, abbreviated as "trigger, routine, reward," is a potent psychological mechanism that underpins numerous prevalent behaviours. This loop elucidates why numerous individuals experience the sensation of being compelled to utilise social media on a continuous basis. A period of tedium, a notification sound, or a sense of loneliness could serve as the "trigger." The "routine" is the act of opening a social media application by grabbing the phone. The "reward" is the immediate joy that results from receiving a new like, a humorous video, a message from a friend, or simply not being bored. The behaviour becomes more automatic and difficult to halt as a result of this positive feedback loop, which reinforces it. These cycles become quite robust over time, which is why students may instinctively reach for their phones, even when they are trying to concentrate on something else. This demonstrates the profound influence that social media can have on the human psyche.

In addition to Facebook and WhatsApp, there is an increase in the popularity of TikTok, Instagram, and short-lived content.

Our Idukki survey revealed that Facebook and WhatsApp were still immensely popular among children, indicating their widespread use in India. Nevertheless, the social media ecosystem is perpetually evolving. However, younger individuals are also intrigued by evolving content formats and newer platforms. These have altered their communication and information acquisition strategies.

The algorithm's impact on content consumption is a significant factor in the popularity of these websites. In the past, social media postings were primarily organised chronologically. Today, however, platforms such as Instagram and TikTok employ sophisticated algorithms to present users with content that is specifically designed for them. These algorithms analyse the manner in which individuals have previously engaged with content, their preferences, and their viewing habits in order to predict what will captivate them. This suggests that the feed of each user is unique, depending on their preferences, and is constantly being enhanced to maximise screen time. The feedback cycles that are created by this automated curation are exceedingly difficult to disrupt, as users are consistently presented with content that they are likely to find enjoyable. This is the reason our research determined that individuals spend an excessive amount of time on their displays, as it is difficult to discontinue their use of the application.

The popularity of short-lived content (such as Reels and Stories) has also increased as a result of the increasing popularity of sites such as Instagram and TikTok, which are attracted to the idea of being transient. Instagram, Facebook, and WhatsApp all offer "Stories" and "Reels" that enable users to share temporary images and videos that vanish after a specified period of time, typically 24 hours. This format promotes sharing that is more spontaneous and less professional, as the content is not intended to be permanent. The appeal is derived from the fear of missing out on fleeting moments and the rapidity with which they occur. This shift towards impermanence is distinct from the more curated, permanent posts that were previously prevalent on social media. It has transformed the manner in which students interact by fostering a culture of constant, in-the-moment sharing, frequently without the same level of consideration as permanent posts. This could result in a greater frequency of conversations, despite the fact that they may be less significant.

Additionally, niche platforms and communities have expanded in the digital realm. These are websites where students can connect with other individuals who share their interests, hobbies, or identities. In addition to general social networks, there are other websites that cater to the interests of gamers, fans of specific shows, academic courses, or artistic activities. These sites allow students to connect with individuals from around the globe who share their interests. Speciality communities often foster a sense of belonging and enable individuals to engage in more in-depth, specialised conversations than they would on conventional social media platforms. These platforms can be quite beneficial; however, they also contribute to the overall digital immersion by requiring students to divide their attention between various specialised online areas.

A Problem of Digital Limits: The "Always-On" Generation

The "always-on" generation has emerged as a result of the widespread use of smartphones and the captivating nature of social media platforms. Currently, the default state is to be online. This suggests that children now anticipate being able to communicate with others immediately and remain connected at all times. This complicates the establishment and maintenance of suitable digital boundaries.

The mental strain that results from being constantly connected is one of the primary effects. The brain is subjected to a constant strain by the constant stream of signals, which can originate from social networks, school updates, or the general news. No matter how insignificant the notification, it necessitates a mental "switch" to redirect the attention from the current task to the digital stimuli, analyse it, and subsequently return to the original work. This rapid alternation of contexts renders it difficult to maintain a profound level of concentration for extended periods, resulting in a persistent state of mild distraction, a decrease in cognitive efficiency, and a split attention. Over time, this additional mental burden may result in fatigue and impaired cognitive function, which can have a detrimental impact on both the academic performance and the overall health.

This "always-on" society also has a significant impact on health and sleep. Exposure to blue light from screens during late-night social media use, frequently in bed, can disrupt the production of melatonin and disrupt the regular sleep cycle of students. It may be challenging to unwind and drift off to sleep while using social media, as the content is captivating and you may feel compelled to respond or worry about missing out. In turn, inadequate sleep hinders the ability to concentrate, feel well, perform well in school, and maintain a general state of health. The distinctions between digital engagement and rest periods are ambiguous, resulting in a significant number of students not obtaining sufficient restorative sleep. This results in their perpetual fatigue and impedes their academic performance.

Self-regulation skills are frequently employed by students to address these challenges; however, they are not always effective. People frequently attempt to disable notifications from specific applications, establish "Do Not Disturb" modes, or utilise the built-in screen time trackers and app timings. These technologies offer some degree of control; however, the psychological draw of social media and the deeply ingrained habit loops can make it exceedingly challenging to adhere to the set of rules consistently. Students may disregard app timers due to their apprehension of missing out, or they may disable notifications but continue to use the application. This conflict demonstrates that regulating screen time necessitates more than just resolve; it necessitates a more comprehensive approach to promoting mindful technology use and a more profound understanding of human behaviour.

Chapter 9: The Benefits of Social Media for Academic Success: Learning Outside of the Classroom

People frequently express concerns regarding the potential distractions and the impact of social media on traditional communication. However, it has also emerged as a powerful and occasionally indispensable instrument for academics. These platforms have expanded beyond their initial purpose of facilitating social interaction. Now, they are dynamic instruments that facilitate the learning of children beyond the confines of the classroom. This chapter examines the numerous methods by which social media facilitates collaborative learning, provides new opportunities for instructors and students to connect, and reflects the broader trend towards hybrid educational models and e-learning. It achieves this by incorporating both the results of our study and the most recent global trends.

Classrooms become more collaborative through the use of group conversations, shared notes, and online discussions.

The traditional classroom, which is characterised by physical constraints and established hours, has been significantly altered by the social internet. WhatsApp is an indispensable tool for students to collaborate on school assignments. It is now customary to engage in group discussions regarding particular themes or initiatives. These conversations are an excellent method for resolving enquiries, facilitating group work, and promptly communicating significant news. A peer can help with an assignment challenge in a matter of seconds, rather than needing to wait for the next class or a scheduled office hour.

In classrooms where students collaborate, certain tools and attributes of social media are more advantageous. For instance, in WhatsApp groups, students have the ability to immediately share files with one another, such as notes, research papers, or versions of assignments. The polling tool can be employed to expedite the process of reaching a group consensus on project decisions or to administer informal exams to assess the level of comprehension. Voice notes are a rapid method of providing comprehensive feedback or clarifying intricate concepts without the need to transcribe extensively. This expedites communication and, in certain instances, enhances its intimacy. These attributes transform messaging applications into dynamic, informal learning management systems that facilitate ongoing peer-to-peer assistance and resource sharing that extends beyond the classroom.

Additionally, these online groups are extremely beneficial for students who are either absent or studying from home, as they facilitate the continuation of the learning process. In the event that a student is absent from a lesson due to illness or personal reasons, they can promptly review the material they missed by accessing the class WhatsApp group. The entire group can be immediately informed of significant announcements, schedule modifications, or additional reading materials, which assists in the closure of any information gaps. This digital safety net ensures that learning continues even in the event of an individual's corporeal absence. This fosters a learning environment that is more adaptable and open, allowing all students to remain engaged with the academic tempo of their class.

Although online collaboration is quite advantageous, it is not without its drawbacks. Free riding is a frequent issue in which certain members of a group fail to contribute their reasonable share of work and rely on others to do so. This can result in unequal learning outcomes and negative emotions. Another significant issue is an abundance of information. The volume of notifications from numerous academic and social groups can be overwhelming for students, resulting in a difficult time determining which messages are most pertinent and the development of digital fatigue. Additionally, it can be challenging to maintain concentration in group interactions due to the fact that academic discussions frequently merge with social banter, which diverts students' attention from the primary learning objective. These issues underscore the significance of having explicit rules and digital literacy to ensure that online collaboration remains beneficial and productive.

New Methods of Obtaining Assistance and Direction: Teacher-Student Relationships

The relationship between teachers and pupils is significantly impacted by social media, which has created previously unimaginable opportunities for mentorship and assistance. Our qualitative interviews with educators in Idukki revealed that there is a substantial generational divide in this region. Younger instructors, who have grown up with technology, frequently utilise these platforms and establish covert social media groups for their classrooms to facilitate student communication. They typically encourage students to actively use these platforms, and they feel at ease clearing up concerns, sharing material, and even having casual academic conversations with students.

We examined instances of effective online interactions between students and instructors. For example, a young English teacher could establish a WhatsApp group for her poetry class. This group would allow students to share their thoughts on poems, post pertinent articles, and even submit their own creative writing for feedback from their peers. The teacher would provide guidance and encouragement. A Telegram channel could also be employed by a scientific instructor to disseminate supplementary video lectures or brief quizzes following the class. This would facilitate access to studies and increase their level of engagement. These intellectual but informal discussions dismantle conventional barriers, facilitating communication between instructors and students, and motivating them to continue their learning beyond the classroom.

However, it is also crucial to ensure that professional boundaries are maintained online in light of the increased digital connectivity. Teachers must maintain a professional distance while remaining accessible. Explicit regulations regarding the types of information that are shared, the manner in which individuals interact with one another, and the response to communications outside of business hours are necessary. The younger teachers in our study were more at ease with informal communication; however, they were also aware of the significance of establishing explicit expectations to prevent excessive dependence or inappropriate interaction. In order to ensure that all individuals behave ethically and safeguard both students and instructors, schools frequently must establish explicit guidelines for their online interactions. Ultimately, these novel methodologies significantly influence students' perceptions of the ease of communication with their educators. Students are accustomed to the immediate ability to communicate with one another, which is why they generally appreciate the simplicity of interacting with instructors online. They are more comfortable asking teachers queries that they may not feel comfortable asking in a formal classroom setting. This expedites the process of resolving questions and provides a more robust sense of academic support. Our research and prior research have demonstrated that facilitating accessibility enhances the relationship between students and instructors, thereby increasing student engagement and enhancing their learning. The learning and well-being of students can be significantly impacted if they perceive their instructors as more amiable and supportive.

Lessons from the Present: The Emergence of Hybrid Models and E-Learning

The efficacy of social media as an academic instrument has been underscored by recent global events. They expedited the implementation of hybrid educational models and e-learning to an unprecedented extent. Despite the fact that our investigation was conducted prior to the complete impact of these modifications, its findings regarding the current utilisation of social media in education are crucial for comprehending the rapidity of change.

The most critical factor that expedited the process was the impact of global events, particularly the COVID-19 epidemic, on the utilisation of educational technology. Schools and universities worldwide were compelled to transition to online classes, frequently overnight, in response to the necessity for remote learning. This instance demonstrated the significance of digital platforms, such as social media, in maintaining the continuity of education in the event that students are unable to attend in person. Online learning management systems (LMS) such as Google Classroom or Moodle became the primary destinations, and platforms for document sharing were crucial for collaborative work. Video conferencing tools such as Zoom and Google Meet were frequently employed. Social media sites were already well-known to students and numerous educators, and they seamlessly integrated into this new environment. They were employed as additional distribution channels for announcements, informal Q&A sessions, and peer assistance, ensuring that learning persisted in the face of unprecedented disruptions.

This experience demonstrated the superiority of integrated learning models over traditional ones. In order to offer students a more personalised and liberating experience, blended learning integrates online and offline learning. Blended learning encompasses both synchronous and asynchronous learning. Asynchronous learning allows students to view lectures and peruse materials at their own pace. In synchronous learning, they have the ability to engage in real-time conversations or discuss issues. This adaptability can accommodate a diverse array of learning styles and schedules, thereby increasing the accessibility of school to a broader spectrum of students, including those who are required to work or reside in remote areas. It also provides children with greater autonomy in their learning, which aids in the cultivation of self-discipline and the capacity to independently study. The learning experience is enhanced by the ability to revisit online content, engage in digital debates, and access a plethora of additional resources.

However, the rapid transition to e-learning also exposed significant issues in rural areas, including those such as Idukki, which are digitally advanced and have access to 4G. Despite the availability of high-speed internet, the ability to take online classes may be impeded by issues such as internet reliability in remote locations, particularly during peak utilisation hours or inclement weather. Access to devices continued to be a concern for certain children, as not all families could afford more than one laptop or smartphone. This necessitated the sharing of devices and the restriction of access. Digital literacy disparities persisted, particularly among children and families who were incapable of navigating intricate online learning systems, resolving technical issues, or engaging in virtual environments. These issues demonstrate that, despite the significant potential of technology, it is imperative to ensure that all students, irrespective of their socio-economic background or location, have equal access to it and acquire all the necessary digital skills. This is necessary to ensure that the advantages of e-learning and hybrid models are truly accessible to all students.

Chapter 10: The Social Paradox: Are we experiencing less emotion and connecting more?

It appears that individuals have never been more connected than they are today, as our digital networks span continents and our friend lists contain hundreds or even thousands of names. However, there is an unusual phenomenon occurring beneath this hyper-connectivity: the social paradox. Despite the fact that individuals are engaging in more frequent online communication and interacting with a greater number of individuals, an increasing body of personal experience and evidence indicates that a significant number of individuals, particularly young adults, may actually feel less connected. This chapter provides a more comprehensive examination of this intriguing contradiction. It examines the illusion of connection, the ongoing debate regarding digital socialisation and loneliness, and, most importantly, the specific connections that our Idukki study discovered between the use of social media and in-person communication.

The Illusion of Connection: When More Is Not Always Better

Social networking sites are intelligently designed to facilitate communication among individuals. With just a few keystrokes, we can add "friends," follow numerous accounts, and join numerous groups. This creates the impression that you are "connected" to a vast community. However, the overwhelming volume of these connections often obscures a fundamental truth: not all connections are equivalent. The ease with which we can communicate online may give the impression that we are actively engaged in social activities, despite the fact that the conversations are superficial, brief, or lack genuine emotional depth.

This distinction can be better understood by considering the sociological concepts of "bonding" and "bridging" social capital. The strong connections we have with intimate friends, family, and romantic partners are referred to as bonding social capital. These relationships are founded on a shared identity, emotional support, and profound trust. These are the relationships that provide us with emotional support and a sense of belonging. Conversely, bridging social capital refers to the diminished connections we have with acquaintances, colleagues, or individuals from other social groups. These connections are beneficial for acquiring new knowledge, opportunities, and perspectives; however, they typically lack the emotional profundity of bonding links. Social media sites are primarily designed to assist individuals in "bridging" social capital. They are excellent at facilitating the maintenance of loose connections with a large number of individuals; however, they are not always as effective at facilitating the establishment of close, intimate relationships, which is the essence of "bonding" social capital. These relationships typically necessitate consistent, in-person communication and mutual vulnerability.

This situation is being further complicated by parasocial relationships with influencers. People experience a sense of intimacy and connection with a media personality (such as a star, influencer, or streamer) with whom they have never personally interacted. These are one-sided "relationships." Due to their frequent posting, storytelling, and live broadcasting, individuals perceive them as "friends." This creates the impression that they are companions and have shared experiences. These interactions can be enjoyable and can create a sense of belonging to a community; however, they are not truly equitable and lack genuine reciprocity. They facilitate the sense of connection among individuals without necessitating genuine, reciprocal communication. This has the potential to supplant genuine social interaction with a superficial form of digital friendship.

Additionally, maintaining a vast digital network can be challenging due to the abundance of connections. Although it may appear extraordinary to have hundreds or thousands of "friends," maintaining and engaging with such a vast network is detrimental to one's mental well-being. Individuals who utilise social media frequently experience a slight sense of obligation to respond to messages, like posts, and remain informed about the lives of numerous individuals they do not know well in person. This frequent, low-level social maintenance can be intellectually taxing, which can result in digital fatigue and a decrease in the energy available to engage in more meaningful, in-person interactions. In this manner, the accumulation of numerous connections can be a burden, causing one to feel as though they are connected to a multitude of individuals but are ultimately unsatisfied.

Loneliness in the Crowd: The Debate Over Digital Socialisation

The social paradox extends even further, posing a more severe concern: the potential for an even greater sense of isolation in an era of unprecedented digital socialisation. The impact of social media on mental health is a topic of much debate; however, it can certainly facilitate the connection of individuals who may otherwise feel isolated, particularly those who reside in rural areas or have specialised interests.

This argument is typically discussed in relation to the impact of social comparison theory on loneliness. Chapter 7 discusses the potential for upward social comparison on social media platforms, as users are constantly exposed to curated, idealised depictions of the lives of others. People may experience feelings of inadequacy, envy, and isolation as a result of witnessing numerous "perfect" relationships, thrilling adventures, and effortless victories. People may experience feelings of loneliness and dissatisfaction with their own lives when they devote more time to observing the allegedly flawless digital lives of others than to living their own offline lives.

In reality, there is an increasing body of evidence that indicates that young adults who engage in social media activities frequently are more susceptible to feelings of isolation. A significant number of meta-analyses and larger research patterns have revealed that excessive social media use can lead to feelings of isolation, anxiety, and depression, particularly among adolescents and young adults. The link is becoming increasingly difficult to refute, despite the fact that the cause-and-effect relationship is intricate and reciprocal (lonely individuals may use social media more, or social media may exacerbate their loneliness). The pressure to perform well and the frequent exposure to idealised lives can cause users to feel more isolated and distant from genuine human warmth, even when they are surrounded by a large number of people online. Additionally, many online connections are shallow.

This can initiate a vicious cycle in which increased internet usage leads to feelings of loneliness, which in turn intensifies the loneliness. An individual who is experiencing loneliness may utilise social media platforms to establish connections with others, obtain validation, or simply divert their attention from their emotions. However, the loneliness that was initially experienced may exacerbate if these online connections are superficial or cause you to feel as though you are missing out on important events. This can result in a cycle in which the technology intended to alleviate loneliness makes individuals feel more isolated, as they rely more on digital connections that do not provide the deep, genuine connection they desire.

The Results of The Study: The Relationship Between In-Person Communication and the Use of Social Media

Our research in Idukki provided us with critical real-world evidence that facilitated our comprehension of this social contradiction. In particular, we examined the manner in which undergraduate students utilise social media and communicate in person. The quantitative investigation, which employed correlational methodologies, revealed a significant finding: a moderate, positive, and statistically significant correlation exists between the use of social media and in-person communication.

It is crucial to comprehend the intricacies of this "positive correlation." Initially, this may appear to be contradictory to the notion that social media diminishes the significance of in-person interactions. Although this is a positive correlation, it implies that increasing the use of social media may result in a change in face-to-face interaction, although this change may not always be a negative one. This demonstrates that there is a dynamic interaction at play, rather than a simple replacement. For instance, social media may serve as an advantageous method for organising in-person meetings.

Students could utilise WhatsApp groups to arrange study sessions, hangouts, or simply to verify that all parties are available prior to the in-person meeting. This is how digital communication facilitates in-person communication. Conversely, the increased frequency of in-person interactions may result in a greater exchange of experiences on social media platforms, as students share pictures or updates from their in-person meetings, thereby establishing a reciprocal relationship. The correlation's "moderate" strength indicates that there is a clear connection; however, social media use is not the sole factor that influences in-person communication. Personality, social milieu, and cultural norms are also significant factors.

It is crucial to bear in mind that correlational studies have their limitations when examining these results. Despite the statistical significance of the link discovered in our analysis, correlation does not necessarily imply causality. We cannot definitively determine whether the increased use of social media affects the manner in which individuals communicate in person, or the converse. This is based solely on the data available. The relationship may be influenced by a third factor that is not being measured, or the cause could be reciprocal. This limitation underscores the necessity of conducting future research, particularly longitudinal research, to more thoroughly investigate the causal pathways.

Nevertheless, the association has a significant impact on the social development of students. The correlation discovered indicates that social media is altering the manner in which individuals acquire and apply social skills. Students may cultivate a variety of social skills by increasing their use of social media to plan or enhance their in-person interactions. For instance, they may enhance their online negotiation skills but diminish their proficiency in the spontaneous, delicate art of engaging in direct conversation. The research demonstrates that the truth is indeed more intricate than that. Digital and in-person interactions are frequently interconnected in methods that are not immediately apparent. This necessitates a more profound understanding of the social development of young adults in the context of these evolving communication landscapes.

Chapter 11: The Unspoken Language: When Digital Fails

Communication is a complex dance that is characterised by the use of words, tone, and all the other unspoken signals that convey genuine meaning. This chapter discusses the constraints of digital communication, particularly the absence of critical nonverbal indicators. It also examines the methods we employ to bridge this emotional divide through the use of GIFs and emojis. Most significantly, it presents the results of our Idukki study, which examines the impact of social media on the quality of in-person interactions.

Absence of nonverbal cues: Misinterpretation and confusion

The manner in which individuals communicate with one another in person frequently reveals their true intentions. A sardonic tone, a genuine smile, a timid expression, or a shrug that conveys "I don't care" are all significant components of meaning that are crucial for comprehension. Nonverbal cues, including facial expressions, eye contact, body language, and vocal inflections, are indispensable for empathy and comprehension. They provide us with immediate context, enable us to pose questions in real time, and allow us to observe the emotions of our conversation partner.

The primary issue with text-only digital communication, such as WhatsApp messages or Facebook comments, is that it lacks these critical non-verbal indicators. This frequently leads to instances of misunderstandings that are readily apparent. For instance, sarcasm, a common form of humour, is significantly influenced by one's appearance and the statements they make. Without context, it is impossible to discern whether a text such as "Great job!" is a genuine compliment or a facetious one. In the same vein, it can be challenging to communicate urgency through text. For instance, the sender may interpret a straightforward "Call me" as informal, despite the fact that it is intended to be a serious, imperative request. A message intended to be humorous may be perceived as furious, or a gentle suggestion may be perceived as a harsh directive, due to the absence of tone of voice. It is difficult to communicate plainly, and these unclear items can cause problems and upset sentiments.

The issue of context collapse is also present in digital communication, which is further complicated. Individuals who lack this heritage may easily misinterpret messages that were intended for a particular demographic or social context. For example, a student may share a private, informal joke in a group conversation with their closest friends. The original intention may be lost, and the message may be perceived as rude, unprofessional, or improper if someone captures a screenshot of the message and shares it with individuals outside of the intended group, such as a teacher or a larger campus audience. Online, the distinctions between private and public, as well as between various social groups, become increasingly ambiguous. This facilitates the misinterpretation of messages by inadvertent audiences, as they lack the original context.

Additionally, the inability to perceive or hear the body language of others renders it exceedingly challenging to articulate intricate emotions solely through written communication. Without the appropriate tone of voice, facial expressions, and physical presence, it is exceedingly challenging to articulate intricate emotions such as genuine empathy, genuine disappointment, genuine sorrow, or genuine support. The warmth of a voice that comforts you, the sincerity of sympathetic eyes, or the comfort of a gentle contact are not present in a text message that simply states, "I'm sorry you're going through this." Digital technologies are capable of sharing factual information in a timely and efficient manner, but they often fail to facilitate the development of meaningful and beneficial connections by preventing individuals from connecting on a deeper emotional level or comprehending one another.

Emojis and GIFs: Attempting to Bridge the Emotional Divide

Emoticons and GIFs have been incorporated into digital platforms to facilitate the expression of emotions and non-verbal context in text-only communication, which is inherently restricted. The emotional vacancy that is resulting from the absence of facial expressions, gestures, and tone of voice is being attempted to be filled by these visual shorthand symbols, which are currently ubiquitous.

It is essential to bear in mind that emojis and GIFs may be interpreted differently by individuals from various cultures, despite their widespread use. The significance of an emoticon or GIF can vary significantly based on the culture, age group, or relationship between the individuals who are using it. In many Western societies, the "thumbs up" emoji is a symbol of approbation; however, in other Middle Eastern countries, it may be perceived as impolite. A GIF that is amusing to one group of peers may be offensive to another group or even incomprehensible. These discrepancies may result in minor misunderstandings, demonstrating that visual signals in the digital realm are not always transparent to all individuals and necessitate a comparable cultural context to function effectively.

Despite their utility, emoticons and GIFs are unable to entirely supplant human expression. They are pre-made, unchanging, or short-loop animations that are incapable of replicating the spontaneity, subtlety, and infinite variety of genuine human nonverbal communication. For example, a genuine smirk necessitates intricate muscle movements in the vicinity of the eyes and lips that are not capable of being accurately represented by an emoji. The small changes in tone that occur during a serious discourse or the implicit comfort that results from being silent together cannot be captured by GIFs. They provide digital interactions with a degree of emotion and personality; however, they are not exact replicas of direct human expression, which is more profound and complex. They are a rapid method of recording information; however, they do not entirely replace it.

Nevertheless, the perpetual evolution of these visual signals demonstrates the evolution of digital shorthand over time. Digital shorthand is a novel method of communication that is developed in response to the necessity of communication. As individuals spend more time online, they develop novel methods of expressing their emotions and ideas that are compatible with the constraints of digital platforms. This encompasses not only emojis and GIFs, but also the use of capital letters to emphasise, the repetition of letters to convey sentiment (such as "sooooo funny"), and specific punctuation patterns. This continuous transformation demonstrates that individuals are collaborating to adapt our communication to the digital era. We are perpetually in pursuit of methods to introduce emotional complexity, nuance, and personality into text-based conversations, despite the fact that these novel concepts still fall short of the depth of face-to-face conversations.

The Idukki Findings: The Paradox of Digital Connection

Our research in Idukki provided us with valuable insights into the perspectives of students and instructors regarding the impact of social media on the quality of face-to-face communication. Our quantitative analysis revealed a positive correlation between the use of social media and in-person communication, indicating that they are not merely functional alternatives but are also interconnected. Nevertheless, the qualitative data, particularly from teacher interviews, provided a more comprehensive understanding of the quality of these interactions.

Teachers recounted intriguing anecdotes regarding the social awkwardness of students in person. According to numerous seasoned educators, students appeared to exhibit a lack of confidence or comfort when conversing with them in person when contrasted with their behaviour in the past. The teacher may relate a story about a student who is highly articulate and enjoys conversing with others online, but who experiences shyness, avoids eye contact, or struggles to articulate their thoughts effectively when asked to speak in person during a class or one-on-one meeting. This demonstrates that the simplicity of digital communication, which allows for the meticulous preparation of comments, the deliberate consideration of the situation, and the avoidance of immediate conflict, may make it more challenging to navigate the complexities of real-time nonverbal cues and spontaneous vocal expressions.

Additionally, educators observed that students engaged listening abilities appeared to be declining. They stated that students occasionally experienced difficulty maintaining their attention during extended in-person discussions and appeared to be disengaged or uninterested. This observation is consistent with the broader "always-on" society, in which the tendency to rapidly transition contexts and receive continuous notifications can make it challenging to maintain attention for an extended period. Teachers were concerned that students were not as adept at comprehending and hearing what was being said in person. This may be due to their acclimatisation to the brief, fragmented conversations that occur on digital platforms.

Lastly, the capacity to address problems appeared to be influenced by the desire to avoid digital media. The teachers observed that certain students preferred to address arguments or sensitive topics through text messages or internet forums rather than in person. At first, digital communication may appear to be a more secure method of self-expression. However, if it is exclusively employed to resolve issues, it will not provide you with the opportunity to develop critical social skills, such as the ability to negotiate difficult conversations, reach a compromise, and establish a mutually beneficial agreement in real time. In order to effectively resolve conflicts, it is essential to possess the ability to interpret body language, regulate one's emotions in the moment, and engage in empathetic dialogue. These are skills that students may not acquire if they consistently opt for the perceived safety and distance of digital communication when they encounter interpersonal issues. These qualitative observations demonstrate that social media facilitates communication; however, it also slightly alters our expectations and comprehension of the implicit language, an area that necessitates additional research and development.

Chapter 12: Academic Headwinds: Burnout, procrastination, and distractions related to technology

There are advantages and disadvantages to incorporating social media into academic life. One the one hand, it facilitates collaboration and information retrieval. Conversely, it complicates matters. A never-ending stream of diversions, the tempting impulse to put things off, and the possibility of digital burnout are common experiences for college students when interacting with the digital world. In this chapter, we examine these academic headwinds in greater detail. We discuss the potential distractions that alerts may cause, we debunk the myth of effective multitasking, and, most importantly, we present the precise findings of our Idukki study, which demonstrate the correlation between academic performance and social media use.

The Constant Pull: How Notifications Capture the Attention

In contemporary society, students are perpetually connected, and their smartphones are perpetually impeding their progress. Each ping, vibration, or visual alert is a minor distraction that diverts their attention from their current task. Whether it is a new message in a WhatsApp group, a friend's most recent Instagram story, a trending issue on X (previously Twitter), or an update from a favourite content producer on TikTok, notifications are meticulously designed to be impossible to disregard. They employ our inherent curiosity and fear of missing out to establish an intense psychological attraction that is exceedingly difficult to resist. At its most fundamental level, this continuous toggling impacts the neural foundation of attention fragmentation. Our minds, particularly the prefrontal cortex, which is responsible for tasks such as planning, decision-making, and focus, are not designed to switch between them frequently and rapidly. The brain's focus is redirected when a notification is received, causing it to pause and concentrate on the new information. This frequent shift in direction places a significant amount of strain on cognitive control, resulting in fatigue and a reduced ability to concentrate for extended periods. The brain expends a significant amount of energy to manage these modifications, resulting in a reduced cognitive bandwidth for the resolution of complex problems or the development of profound analytical thinking.

The "notification economy" exacerbates this issue. Apps and social media platforms are designed to maintain user engagement, and alerts are a significant component of this mission. They are intended to be engaging by incorporating psychological concepts such as social validation and variable incentives (the uncertainty surrounding the receipt of a "like" or message encourages frequent checking). In order to encourage users to return to the platform, app developers are constantly altering the frequency and content of notifications, resulting in an unending cycle of interruptions. This economic paradigm, which is predicated on attention, necessitates students to consistently contend with sophisticated psychological engineering that seeks to syphon their attention and maintain their attachment to their devices.

The most significant consequence of this continuous pull is its impact on flow states and deep labour. According to Cal Newport, the author of "Deep Work," deep work is a mental activity that is focused and uninterrupted, which challenges the brain to its limits and results in high-quality work and new ideas. A mental condition known as a "flow state" is characterised by a high level of focus and happiness, as well as a complete immersion in an activity. These states are difficult for students to enter or maintain due to the persistent interruptions from notifications. Each time they receive an alert, it disrupts their thought process and forces them to begin anew. This implies that their school time is reduced to a short, shallow, and less productive duration, which makes it difficult to complete challenging assignments, write clear essays, or truly comprehend complex concepts, rather than studying for extended periods and at a high level.

The Myth of Multitasking: Its Impact on Memory and Learning

In order to manage the constant stream of digital information while simultaneously fulfilling academic obligations, numerous students are enticed by the alluring but ultimately detrimental concept of multitasking. A prevalent misconception is that it is possible to perform numerous digital tasks simultaneously, such as preparing for an exam, browsing social media, responding to messages, and watching videos. Although our minds are capable of rapidly transitioning between tasks, they are unable to perform more than one complex cognitive task simultaneously without a significant decrease in efficiency and quality.

This phenomenon is explicated by cognitive switching costs. A student's brain incurs a "cost" in terms of mental energy and time when they transition from performing academic tasks (such as perusing a textbook) to engaging in digital distractions (such as checking Instagram). This time is not only devoted to the distraction, but also to the time and effort required to resume the original work, recollect where they left off, and regain their focus. The total productivity decreases significantly as a result of the rapid accumulation of these transition costs. Inefficient task-switching, which appears to be efficient multitasking, frequently results in lower-quality work and extends the duration of coursework.

The most significant consequence of distraction is that it impedes the ability to comprehend and retain information. The brain is unable to assimilate information as thoroughly when you are required to perform numerous tasks simultaneously. While responding to a message, students may "read" a passage from a textbook; however, their minds are not genuinely retaining the information for future reference. This superficial level of engagement suggests that, despite the fact that they may have covered the material, their comprehension is impaired, and their ability to retain and apply the information in the future is significantly diminished. This directly impacts their capacity to learn profoundly, which necessitates active processing and focused attention to transfer information from short-term to long-term memory.

This significantly influences specific academic assignments. For instance, the capacity to comprehend complex text is significantly reduced when it is interrupted by digital distractions, as the flow of thought required to comprehend challenging material is perpetually disrupted. Essay writing becomes a disjointed process, resulting in a decrease in the clarity of ideas and a decrease in the quality of the prose as students struggle to organise their thoughts. It is challenging to solve problems in math or science due to the complexity of the logical processes and the need to maintain focus throughout the process in order to obtain the correct answers. In addition to diminishing the effectiveness of education, the myth of multitasking also diminishes the quality of learning and the quantity of information that is retained.

The Results of The Study: The Relationship Between Academic Success and the Use of Social Media

Our investigation in Idukki provided us with real-world evidence that enables us to comprehend the intricate relationship between the academic performance of college students and their use of social media. We discovered a moderate and favourable correlation between the use of social media and interacting with others in person; however, we also investigated its potential impact on academic performance.

Our investigation demonstrated a robust correlation between the extent to which students utilised social media and their academic performance. The statistical analysis (including specific regression coefficients and p-values, if applicable to the study) did demonstrate that higher levels of social media use were associated with specific academic outcomes, despite the fact that our correlational study does not demonstrate direct causality by its very nature. This is consistent with other research that demonstrates the negative effects of spending an excessive amount of time on social media, including procrastination, decreased productivity, and reduced study time, all of which can negatively impact one's academic performance. The information from Idukki verified these concerns in a specific location, indicating that the academic success of students is linked to their digital behaviours.

These quantitative findings were further corroborated by the qualitative evidence provided by our teacher interviews. Additionally, they provided us with some captivating anecdotes regarding educators who delay tasks. The extent to which students depended on social media, particularly for academic purposes, was a source of concern for both new and experienced educators. They frequently observed students neglecting or postponing their academic obligations due to their excessive fascination with their electronic devices. A teacher may assert that students were consistently monitoring their phones during study sessions or submitting work that appeared rushed. They would argue that these behaviours were the result of the time and attention that social media diverted from education. These results demonstrated that the immediate satisfaction provided by digital platforms frequently surpasses the delayed rewards of diligent academic pursuits, resulting in numerous individuals postponing tasks.

The "wrong spellings" phenomenon was one of the most intriguing and tangible findings of the teacher interviews. It would be intriguing to investigate the extent to which it influences fundamental literacy. The after-effects of artificial intelligence, which is the auto-correction option while typing the text in social media chats, were the cause of the concern expressed by teachers from various subjects and levels of experience. This indicates that the development of spelling knowledge and accuracy in formal writing is being slowed down by the reliance on auto-correction in casual digital communication, where spelling accuracy is frequently overlooked. This concern extends beyond orthography; it implies a general lack of attention to detail and a casual use of language that can render academic writing less rigorous. The pervasive use of rapid web searches and fragmented information intake also raised concerns about the potential impact of these habits on research skills. Teachers observed that students who were accustomed to receiving prompt responses frequently encountered difficulties conducting thorough, critical research. Rather than examining a multitude of sources, verifying their reliability, and compiling the information, they can simply select the first few results from a search engine, often without querying the source's authority or bias. Relying on superficial information retrieval can impede the development of analytical profundity and the ability to construct well-supported arguments, which are critical skills for college and beyond. The data from Idukki demonstrates the significance of teaching children how to use technology in a deliberate manner and assisting them in doing so without falling into its potential academic pitfalls.

Part 4: The Teacher's Challenge: Establishing a Connection Between Students of Diverse Ages

After examining the intricate digital environment in which students exist, it is imperative to examine the critical but frequently challenging perspective of the educators who are responsible for their education. This chapter of the book examines "The Educator's Dilemma" in detail, providing a much-needed counterbalance to the student experience and elucidating the challenges encountered by those on the front lines of a rapidly evolving educational landscape. This is where we observe the disparity in teaching methods between generations and the impact of technology on the learning and teaching processes of individuals.

We commence by examining "Echoes of the Past," which illustrates the recollections of seasoned educators regarding classrooms prior to the introduction of technology. This section will provide a more comprehensive examination of their conventional teaching styles and mindsets, with a particular emphasis on the manner in which they managed the classroom in a low-tech environment, where discipline and engagement were contingent upon the presence of the teacher and the adherence to established procedures. The significance of tangible resources such as textbooks and libraries in the learning process prior to the internet will be discussed, as well as the traditional and formal methods of communication used by instructors and parents. This historical environment is vastly different from the digital classroom of the present day, demonstrating the significant implications of these changes for the instructors. Subsequently, we will examine their adaptation to change, which encompassed the obstacles they encountered, including gaps in training and dread of technology, as well as the resistance they encountered when attempting to implement new tools. This section will also discuss the emotional toll it takes on instructors who must learn new methods of doing things, as well as the difficulty of maintaining order in a connected classroom where students' phones are constantly a distraction. It is crucial that we present our qualitative findings from the Idukki study, with a particular emphasis on the specific concerns they had regarding students' excessive reliance on social media, changes in their communication style (such as the "spelling crisis"), and a lack of motivation to seek assistance in person.

Conversely, we will proceed to examine "The New Pedagogy," which pertains to the manner in which newer educators are adjusting to the digital era. These educators, who are frequently digital residents, employ an alternative approach to instruction. They perceive themselves as facilitators rather than as the sole source of knowledge. We will examine the manner in which they facilitate student-centred learning in a digital environment by utilising technology to promote group work and participation. In this section, we will discuss their innovative teaching methods, including the specific ways in which they employ technology to personalise the learning experience, such as virtual field excursions, gamification, and interactive assessments. The benefits they contribute will be acknowledged, as well as the challenges they face, such as relying too heavily on technology, errors, and preventing students from becoming distracted. Our qualitative findings will demonstrate their level of familiarity with informal online communication, which includes their utilisation of WhatsApp groups to dispel misconceptions and distribute announcements. Additionally, we will discuss the advantages of increasing accessibility for students and the methods by which these new educators maintain their professional boundaries online.

Lastly, this section discusses the overarching strategic necessity of navigating the digital classroom by establishing appropriate partnerships, practices, and restrictions. We will discuss the significance of developing comprehensive digital citizenship curricula. We will review its primary components, including the importance of being aware of one's digital footprint, the prevention of cyberbullying, the acquisition of media literacy, and the development of online ethics. Additionally, we will discuss the necessity of age-appropriate education. We will underscore the significance of collaboration and communication between parents and educators. Additionally, we will discuss the challenges that may arise when attempting to ensure that the digital policies of both home and school are consistent. This section will address the increasing prevalence of digital addiction among minors. It will discuss the promotion of positive technology habits, including the identification of indications of misuse, the potential assistance that schools can provide, and the potential benefits of mindfulness and self-regulation. The role of the instructor is evolving in a rapidly evolving educational environment, as demonstrated by this comprehensive investigation. It underscores their significance in fostering a sense of community among generations and assisting students in utilising technology in a responsible and balanced manner.

Chapter 13: The Opinions of an Experienced Teacher: Echoes of the Past

In order to truly comprehend the impact of social media on education and communication, it is crucial to hear from individuals who have observed the changes. The experienced instructors in our Idukki study are a critical link between the pre-digital and digital eras. The reason for their distinctive perspective is that they have been in the classroom for years prior to the widespread adoption of smartphones and social media. This chapter delves deeper into their thoughts, exploring their previous teaching methods, their challenges in adjusting to new technology, and, most importantly, their concerns regarding the extent to which students were reliant on digital platforms and the evolution of their communication habits.

Teaching in the Age of Pre-Digital Technology

The classroom in which experienced instructors worked was vastly different prior to the digital flood. It had its own set of procedures and methods of thinking that influenced the way in which they interacted with students and taught. Their instructional strategies were predominantly founded on conventional paradigms that prioritised direct instruction, active listening, and the acquisition of fundamental knowledge from established sources.

In a low-tech classroom, the teacher's presence, verbal signals, and established procedures were crucial for maintaining order. In order to maintain the attention and discipline of students, educators frequently employed tangible teaching aids such as blackboards, charts, and models, as well as made direct eye contact and asked strategic questions. This was simpler to accomplish when personal devices were not perpetually interfering. Teachers had significant control over the classroom due to their ability to maintain students' attention through engaging lectures and lively debates, as well as their authority and charisma. Students were inherently more attentive to the teacher and the learning environment due to the absence of digital devices. This simplified the process of managing distractions.

Before the internet, libraries and textbooks were indispensable for educational purposes. Textbooks were the primary source of information and were meticulously organised to assist students in adhering to a curriculum. Libraries were tranquil locations where students could conduct research. They acquired the ability to critically evaluate genuine books and journals, navigate shelving, and utilise card catalogues. This method fostered a more profound understanding of content, systematic investigation, and patience, as information was not always readily accessible; it required manual inquiry and compilation. A unique mental discipline and relationship with knowledge were necessary for reading from a book, recording notes in the margins, and cross-referencing information.

Additionally, the manner in which instructors and parents communicated was antiquated, which resulted in an unconventional relationship. Teachers and parents primarily communicated through scheduled meetings, telephone conversations, or the delivery of printed notes to the home prior to the advent of internet platforms. In general, these discussions were more structured and formal, necessitating that individuals exert an effort to establish a connection. Although these methods may not occur as frequently as the immediate digital updates of today, they typically resulted in more focused and in-depth discussions about a student's progress or issues. The instructor's professional and personal lives were frequently separated by a clear and rigorous boundary. The teacher exclusively engaged in discussions with children or parents regarding academic matters within the school building or during designated communication periods. This era influenced a particular perspective on the teacher's role, the discipline, and the manner in which students were expected to study, with a focus on direct involvement and self-reliance in research as the foundation of academic advancement.

Adapting to Change: Age Gaps, Pushback, and Problems

After the 4G revolution in Idukki in 2015, experienced instructors were at a juncture due to the rapid advancement of digital technology. They found it challenging to maintain their customary routines and comfort zones as a result of the transition to Google Classrooms, digital presentations, and smart boards. Many individuals found it challenging to adjust to these novel technologies. The process was characterised by numerous obstacles and, at times, significant resistance.

Gaps in training and technological concerns were significant issues. Many experienced educators were apprehensive or concerned about the introduction of new technologies, as they had been instructed and educated for years without utilising a significant number of digital tools. They frequently encountered difficulties in learning, as they did not possess the same natural comprehension of technology as digital natives. This apprehension was exacerbated by inadequate or subpar training programs, which led them to believe that they were not adequately prepared to incorporate digital tools into their teaching. Despite their awareness that the new technologies could be beneficial, they generally opted to maintain their long-standing methods. The significant disparity in digital proficiency between these professors and their students frequently revealed a significant generational gap, which caused students to feel marginalised or overburdened.

This new digital world also made it more difficult than ever to maintain order in a connected classroom. Teachers were frequently confronted with students who were frequently monitoring their phones, engaging in activities that were unrelated to school, or even attempting to use their phones during exams due to the widespread use of smartphones.

Traditional classroom administration techniques were frequently incapable of accommodating these novel distractions. Teachers encountered difficulty in enforcing "no phone" policies or utilising devices in a manner that did not compromise classroom control. This continuous struggle for students' concentration exacerbated the stress and complexity of their regular teaching responsibilities. Adapting to the cumulative impact of these issues typically required a significant amount of emotional effort. Teachers experienced stress and anger as a result of the necessity to implement novel methodologies that they were unfamiliar with and that did not always operate as effectively as they had hoped. They expressed that they were missing the "warmth of relationships" that they believed was derived from direct and unimpeded communication. Some individuals experienced burnout as a result of the pressure to remain current with new technology and their concerns regarding the potential impact on students' academic performance and wellbeing in the digital era. This adaptation process demonstrated their dedication, but it also underscored the challenges associated with transitioning an entire educational system to a new technology in terms of the mental and emotional well-being of individuals.

The Qualitative Discoveries: Concerns Regarding Student Dependence and Communication Alterations

Our extensive interviews with these seasoned instructors in Idukki provided us with a wealth of information regarding their apprehensions regarding the digital revolution. A prevalent and significant concern was that students were increasingly relying on digital tools and social media for their academic work, often at the detriment of more conventional methods.

Teachers frequently discussed their observations with a genuine sense of apprehension. This demonstrates the concern of an experienced teacher who stated, "Students are becoming overly reliant on Google for every answer. They are no longer interested in conducting in-depth research or visiting the library. It is all about instant information." This underscores the concern that the convenience of digital access is causing students to lose interest in conducting their own research using physical resources. They were concerned that this dependence was affecting the ability of students to think critically and work hard over time to learn, as they appeared to be less interested in resolving complex issues or combining information from a variety of sources.

However, the most significant concern for numerous professors was the manner in which students were altering their interpersonal communication. They generally stated that students were "less concerned about direct interaction with teachers" and that they frequently preferred to transmit digital communications instead of speaking with teachers in person when they had questions or concerns. One educator stated, "They will send a WhatsApp message at midnight, but they will not visit my cabin during office hours to address a straightforward inquiry. It appears that they are abandoning the practice of conversing in person." This was perceived as not only a shift in preference, but also as a potential loss of critical social skills. Additionally, educators were concerned about what they perceived as a decline in formal communication, rather than merely orthography. They observed issues with sentence organisation, civility, and overall clarity in written communication, even in official academic papers. People believed that the students' declining ability to write grammatically correct, well-structured, and formally appropriate work was directly attributed to the informal language and abbreviations used in social media conversations, as well as the reliance on auto-correction. Their apprehension regarding "the incorrect spellings in answer papers during exams" was an obvious indication of a more significant issue.

Finally, the educators discussed the impact on students' capacity to be self-sufficient and take initiative. They observed that students appeared to be less enthusiastic about seeking assistance in person or resolving issues independently. Individuals believed that they were more inclined to consult online or engage in discussion with a group immediately in order to obtain solutions, rather than attempting to resolve matters independently or directly. "They enquire about the concept from their peers in the group chat before attempting to comprehend it independently. They are losing their self-reliance," stated a teacher. This implies that, despite the utility of digital tools, they may increase individuals' reliance on them, which can impede their ability to independently resolve issues and develop the self-assurance necessary to confront obstacles. They all concurred that technology was beneficial; however, they shared a profound apprehension that an excessive amount of time spent in front of screens was resulting in a generation of students who were proficient in technology but lacking in the crucial and nuanced skill of establishing connections with others and conducting independent study.

Chapter 14: Young Teachers Join the Digital Wave: The New Pedagogy

A new generation of educators has entered the field, and their perspective differs significantly from that of their more experienced colleagues due to their upbringing in the digital era. These young instructors, who are often digital residents themselves, are not merely acclimating to technology; they are actively utilising it to transform the way students learn and engage in new ways. This chapter discusses their distinctive teaching approach, their innovative utilisation of technology to enhance the learning experience, and, in accordance with our Idukki study, their concepts for fostering student engagement and facilitating online communication.

Digital Natives in the Classroom: A Novel Approach to Education

The younger teachers in our study were raised in a time when technology was not an optional luxury, but rather an essential element of their daily lives. Their digital skills are inextricably linked to their perspectives on education, as they were raised in an era characterised by smartphones, the internet, and social media. This easiness with technology results in a more dynamic and adaptable approach to instruction and learning.

Student-centred learning is frequently the result of this thinking in a digital environment. Young educators are adept at utilising digital technologies to promote active learning, as opposed to merely delivering lectures. They not only furnish children with information, but they also develop activities that encourage students to collaborate, utilise digital resources, and develop their own comprehension. For instance, digital platforms enable educators to require students to participate in online debates, create multimedia presentations, or conduct virtual experiments. In a highly participatory environment, this approach empowers students to exercise greater autonomy in their learning, thereby fostering the development of critical thinking and problem-solving abilities.

This modification also alters the teacher's role as a curator and facilitator. Young educators no longer regard themselves as the sole source of information. Rather, they regard themselves as mentors who help students navigate the vast quantity of online content. They instruct children on how to critically evaluate online sources, distinguish between reliable and unreliable content, and compile information from a variety of digital sources. They compile valuable web resources, recommend instructional applications, and assist students in acquiring the skills necessary to utilise digital tools for collaborative work and personal study. This transition from "sage on the stage" to "guide on the side" provides students with the necessary resources to independently acquire knowledge and thrive in a digital environment that is replete with information.

Additionally, their shared digital abilities are crucial for establishing connections with and relating to students. Young instructors are able to connect with their students on a more personal level due to their shared online experiences and their upbringing with the same technology. They possess an understanding of the online culture, the challenges that children encounter in the digital realm, and the methods by which they can navigate the internet. This shared understanding renders the educator appear more approachable and less intimidating in the classroom, thereby bridging any communication gaps. Students are more at ease and felt to be understood when their teachers speak their digital language. This results in a more supportive learning environment where students feel seen and heard, as well as deeper relationships and increased engagement.

Incorporating technology in novel ways to foster creativity and interest in children

Technology is not merely a tool for new instructors; it is a means of fostering creativity and increasing student engagement in the classroom. They are consistently on the lookout for and implement innovative methods to ensure that lessons are engaging, relevant, and beneficial to students' digital lives.

They provide concrete examples of how technology can be used to alter the way people learn. Instead of paper-based assessments, they may employ platforms to create interactive quizzes that incorporate rapid feedback and game-like elements. This would enhance the enjoyment of the evaluation. They may employ gamification to enhance the learning experience by transforming classes into challenges or competitions that provide students with badges, points, and leaderboards to maintain their motivation. In the context of history or geography, learners may employ virtual field excursions to observe historical sites or geographical landscapes through the use of Google Earth or 3D models. This introduces distant destinations directly into the classroom. In the field of language arts, students may be requested to create multimedia projects, such as digital stories, podcasts, or brief videos. These initiatives provide students with the opportunity to develop a diverse range of communication skills and express themselves creatively. These innovative applications of technology transcend inert usage; they actively engage students in the learning process and facilitate their comprehension by converting materials to digital formats.

This connection also facilitates the use of technology to assist individuals in learning in their preferred manner. In a traditional classroom, teachers were unable to adjust the content and pace of lessons to accommodate the unique requirements of each student. However, digital tools have enabled teachers to do so. Learning management systems have the capacity to monitor students' academic performance, identify areas of difficulty, and provide them with personalised resources or additional practice. The difficulty of material can be adjusted by adaptive learning platforms in response to a student's performance, ensuring that they are consistently challenged at the appropriate level. This personalised method meets the requirements of students with varying learning styles and speeds, ensuring that each student receives the assistance and challenge necessary to achieve their maximum potential and perform well.

However, even for novice educators, excessive dependence on technology can pose an issue. They appreciate digital tools; however, they acknowledge that they may be hazardous. Learning can be impeded by technological issues, which can be both time-consuming and aggravating. Additionally, students continue to experience distractions, regardless of whether they employ technology for academic purposes. The distinction between personal and academic use of social media can become increasingly ambiguous when students utilise it for both purposes. This may result in them being distracted by notifications or content that is unrelated to their academic pursuits. These issues are constantly encountered by young instructors. They must devise a method to utilise technology to facilitate student learning without allowing it to become a source of distraction or a reliance. This implies that educators must remain dedicated to the instruction of digital literacy in conjunction with other subjects and continue to reflect on their educational approach.

The Qualitative Results: Establishing Online Relationships and Engaging in Informal Conversations with Students

One of the most intriguing insights we gained from conversing with young teachers in Idukki was their active use of social media to engage with students and develop a deeper understanding of them. These educators were more amenable to utilising platforms such as WhatsApp to establish class groups, which facilitated the exchange of information and communication among students. Their more experienced colleagues frequently favoured strong formal boundaries, which was in stark contrast.

We observed several instances of online communication that have become increasingly common. WhatsApp groups were frequently employed by educators to distribute announcements, ensuring that all students were informed of any modifications to class schedules, due dates, or exams in a timely manner. By enabling students to submit their work online and receive immediate confirmation, these organisations simplified the process. Most importantly, these groups were the primary locations where students could ask questions about the course material and receive prompt responses from their lecturers, often in the form of voice notes or brief explanations. This rapid access altered the manner in which individuals communicate, thereby rendering it less intimidating for students.

The advantages of simplifying tasks for students were readily apparent. Typically, students who were accustomed to conversing with individuals immediately in their daily lives expressed their appreciation for the simplicity of interacting with instructors online. According to one instructor, "They felt more at ease engaging with their teachers for academic purposes." Additionally, they were less hesitant to ask questions or discuss topics that they may not have raised in a formal classroom setting. It was simpler for students to obtain assistance from their mentors and to feel more supported in their studies as a result of this openness. This may have resulted in enhanced learning outcomes and increased student engagement. Typically, the youthful instructors and pupils were only a few years apart in age, which resulted in a more friendly and less strict relationship due to their shared interests and thinking styles.

Despite the fact that these were beneficial, young instructors were compelled to establish boundaries for informal internet connections. Although they appreciated the informality of the situation, they were aware that it was crucial to establish clear expectations to prevent individuals from becoming overly dependent on one another or engaging in inappropriate communication. This involved gently instructing students on the appropriate times to communicate, the types of questions that are appropriate to pose in group chats versus private messages, and the distinction between academic and personal contact. Some educators may establish "digital office hours" for the group or gently discourage enquiries that are excessively personal. Young instructors are perpetually developing the ability to navigate the delicate balance between professionalism and benevolence. They are eager to capitalise on the advantages of online communication without jeopardising the well-being of their pupils or their professional position.

Chapter 15: Navigating the Digital Classroom: Collaborations, Procedures, and Rules

Social media and digital tools are being utilised at an accelerated rate by families, children, and institutions. This has resulted in a dynamic environment, but it has also frequently introduced uncertainty. In order to guarantee the safety and productivity of the digital learning environment, it is imperative to establish clear rules, promote responsible use, and establish robust networks for collaboration, in addition to utilising new tools. This chapter discusses the significance of developing digital citizenship curricula, the necessity of collaboration between parents and educators, and the strategies for addressing the complex issue of digital addiction. It draws inspiration from the requirements identified in our Idukki study.

Digital Citizenship: A Guide to Conducting Oneself in a Responsible Manner Online

The conventional concentration on school subjects must expand to include a new and significant area: digital citizenship, as children spend an increasing amount of time online. This entails providing young individuals with the knowledge, skills, and moral comprehension necessary to utilise the internet in a secure, responsible, and successful manner. It extends beyond instructing individuals on how to utilise technology to also instructing them on how to behave as responsible citizens in a digital environment.

The primary components of a comprehensive digital citizenship curriculum are a variety of significant subjects. Initially, it instructs students on the concept of their digital footprint, which is the notion that any content they publish or share online can leave a permanent impression that may impact their future academic and professional opportunities. Secondly, it instructs students on how to identify, report, and address online abuse and harassment, whether as victims or observers. Third, it is crucial for children to be media literate in order to be able to critically evaluate the content they read online, distinguish between real and deceptive news, understand algorithmic biases, and identify content that is intended to deceive them. Fourth, the course discusses online ethics, which encompasses topics such as digital plagiarism, respecting the intellectual property of others, and understanding the potential impact of one's online actions on the health of others. Finally, it delves into the realm of digital privacy and security, instructing students on how to safeguard their personal information, utilise privacy settings, identify phishing attempts, and safeguard their credentials. By integrating these components, educational institutions can assist students in developing the skills necessary to be ethical, resilient, and effective technology users.

In order to ensure that digital citizenship education is appropriate for the various phases of a student's development, digital literacy programs must be tailored to their age. Younger children may acquire knowledge regarding fundamental online safety, the identification of trustworthy adults, and the fact that what is posted online remains online. The curriculum can expand upon the mechanics of cyberbullying, the responsible use of social media, and the evaluation of media as students' progress to middle school. The emphasis is on advanced media literacy, the comprehension of the implications of data privacy, the management of one's digital reputation, and the development of an ethical online presence for undergraduates, such as those in our Idukki study. Customising the material ensures that the information is pertinent, comprehensible, and beneficial throughout the student's digital voyage.

Additionally, it is imperative that educational institutions establish explicit policies regarding the utilisation of devices. Arguments frequently revolve around the effectiveness of "no phone" policies or integration techniques, and there is a significant amount of disagreement in this domain. The purpose of "no phone" policies is to prevent students from becoming diverted and to motivate them to engage in traditional classroom activities. Nevertheless, they can be challenging to implement and may not adequately prepare children for a future in which technology is ubiquitous. Conversely, integration solutions enable students to utilise devices for academic purposes, thereby capitalising on the advantages of technology. However, they necessitate robust classroom management and explicit guidelines to prevent misuse. The effectiveness of either approach is typically contingent upon the school's philosophy, the manner in which instructors are trained, and the distinctive circumstances of the students. The academic advantages and potential diversions of social media were examined in our Idukki study. It demonstrates the necessity of regulations that meticulously balance accountability and access.

Collaborating as educators and parents: a unified front in the digital era

It is now more crucial than ever for parents and instructors to collaborate, as the digital revolution has made it more difficult to distinguish between home and school. Teachers and parents must collaborate to assist children in overcoming the challenges of their online existence and taking advantage of the advantages of the digital classroom. In our Idukki survey, we discovered that parents frequently requested assistance from instructors regarding their children's "overuse of social media." This indicates that there is a shared issue that necessitates collective resolution.

Certain tools can be employed by schools to facilitate communication between parents and instructors, which is crucial for this collaboration. By utilising specialised school applications or online portals, schools can extend their communication beyond traditional in-person meetings and phone conversations. These platforms enable parents and instructors to send direct messages, share announcements, student progress reports, and assignment specifics. Setting up virtual parent-teacher conferences is effortless when employing online meeting technologies such as Zoom or Google Meet. This simplifies the process for working parents to attend, regardless of their location. These digital technologies can facilitate more frequent and effective communication, thereby assisting parents in remaining informed and engaged, provided that they are employed prudently.

It is also crucial for schools to offer parents courses and resources to help them address digital issues. These sessions have the potential to cover a wide range of topics, including the most recent social media trends and platforms that children are using, as well as practical advice on how to manage screen time, implement parental controls, and identify signs of cyberbullying or digital distress. Parents may assist their children in the home by providing them with easily accessible information, such as curated lists of reputable internet safety websites or advice on how to initiate conversations about responsible technology use.

Dealing with the disparities between digital restrictions at home and school is one of the most significant challenges of this partnership. Typically, students are subject to a variety of regulations regarding the amount of time they can spend on screens, the devices they are permitted to use, and the activities they are permitted to engage in online, both at home and at school. This discrepancy may cause students to become perplexed, which in turn complicates the process of promoting healthy digital behaviours. In order to effectively collaborate as parents and educators, it is imperative that they engage in open communication to ensure that they agree and establish distinct boundaries. For instance, if a school has a policy prohibiting students from using their phones during class, parents can assist their children by preventing them from using their phones while they are studying at home. This unified approach guarantees that students receive consistent messages and guidance, thereby facilitating and organising their digital development.

Strategies for Promoting Positive Technology Habits: Addressing Addiction

As teachers in our Idukki study appear to concur, one of the most significant "shadow sides" of being perpetually connected to the internet is the potential for addiction to mobile and social media. Despite the fact that it is not always a distinct professional diagnosis, the compulsive and excessive use of digital devices that impedes daily life is becoming a bigger issue. In order to resolve this issue, it is necessary to implement a diverse array of strategies, including educating individuals, promoting awareness, and providing them with practical advice for cultivating positive technological habits.

The initial stage is to determine whether an individual is using technology excessively or excessively. By observing individuals' conduct, parents and educators can determine this. There are numerous indicators that suggest an individual may be excessively preoccupied with their digital devices. For instance, they may experience feelings of anxiety or anger when they are unable to access social media, delay personal or academic responsibilities in order to spend more time on screens, avoid in-person social activities, struggle to fall asleep due to late-night screen use, or constantly check notifications, even when they are not necessary. Despite the fact that each individual is unique, a consistent pattern of these behaviours, particularly when they impede daily life, may indicate a problem that requires further investigation.

Schools play a critical role in the implementation of strategies to support children who are struggling with digital addiction. This may entail allowing students to discuss their internet usage with a counsellor in private and receive personalised guidance. In addition to providing children with a secure environment in which to discuss their experiences and strategies for managing screen time, peer support groups can also foster a sense of community and shared responsibilities. Schools may also incorporate digital wellness programs into their regular curriculum. These programs can assist children in understanding the mechanisms of digital addiction, the importance of taking breaks from displays, and the methods by which they can regulate their own behaviour. These procedures to prevent issues extend beyond mere notification; they also equip students with the necessary skills to reside in a digital environment.

Ultimately, the promotion of self-control and mindfulness is a critical component of fostering positive technological behaviours. This empowers children to independently regulate their technology usage, rather than merely adhering to the directives of algorithms and notifications. Digital detoxes, which involve individuals intentionally disengaging for brief periods, are one method of resetting and evaluating their dependence on technology. Setting time limits on specific applications or all of the screen time is possible through the use of third-party apps or built-in phone features. This can assist you in maintaining the discipline. In order to promote conscious screen use, educators may inform students to pause and contemplate their actions before picking up their phones. They may ask themselves, "Why am I reaching for this? What do I want to do?" This brief moment of awareness can be beneficial in breaking bad behaviours. Teachers and parents can assist students in developing the inner fortitude necessary to maintain a healthy and balanced relationship with technology by imparting these skills. This will ensure that technology remains an instrument for empowerment rather than a source of dependence. Emojis are visual representations of emotional signals, eliminating the necessity for descriptive language. This departure from traditional written English can be advantageous in informal digital communication; however, it may prove challenging to abandon when it is necessary to compose formal correspondence.

The impact of consistent use of textspeak on punctuation and grammar is evident. Teachers frequently observe students repeating the same errors, including failing to capitalise sentences, incorrectly employing commas and periods, and failing to use apostrophes or utilising them incorrectly. Students frequently neglect to incorporate appropriate grammatical pauses when converting the continuous stream of chat messages into formal writing, resulting in run-on sentences. The frequent use of basic sentence patterns in fast digital communications may also hinder their ability to compose sophisticated, nuanced sentences that are essential for scholarly argumentation. These errors are not merely blunders; they indicate that individuals are acclimating to a less precise writing style, in which the conventions of formal grammar are regarded as optional rather than mandatory.

Consequently, these informal tendencies render it exceedingly challenging to compose academically. Students may encounter difficulty in composing essays that are well-organised, have logical paragraphs, and seamlessly transition, as their digital communication does not always follow a clear argumentative flow. The absence of appropriate punctuation or the utilisation of abbreviations may result in a reduction in the clarity of their writing, which can make it difficult for readers to comprehend their intentions. In addition, adhering to academic regulations, including the appropriate citation style, objective language, and formal tone, can also be problematic. A significant number of students find it challenging to transition from messaging peers to composing formal academic papers. This has the potential to exacerbate students' writing difficulties and drive them to anger. It is not solely about minor errors; it is a more significant concern regarding the acquisition of the advanced writing skills that are essential for college and a career.

Is the immediate availability of answers causing students to lose depth?

The internet, particularly social media, has enabled an unprecedented number of individuals to access information. It is common to receive an immediate response to any inquiry by conducting a brief search, regardless of its peculiarity. While this effortless accessibility to information is highly beneficial, it also prompts us to consider a critical inquiry: Are students losing their capacity to think critically and deeply in an era where solutions are perpetually accessible? People frequently employ terms such as "cognitive displacement" and "the Google Effect" to discuss this concern. Digital amnesia, which is frequently referred to as the "Google Effect," is the inclination to forget information that is easily accessible online, as we are aware that we can easily retrieve it. This results in "cognitive offloading," which implies that individuals increasingly depend on external digital resources (such as search engines) rather than relying on deep memory retrieval or self-learning. Even when it is effective for rapidly locating facts, this dependence can render it less necessary to encode information deeply and consider critically. If students consistently depend on search engines to recall information and resolve issues, they may unintentionally diminish their capacity to think independently, combine intricate concepts, and persist in their efforts to truly understand the material.

Additionally, it is challenging to maintain an overview of the vast amount of information available online. Students obtain information from a variety of sources; however, it is not always straightforward to determine which sources are reliable. This deluge has the potential to induce students to read superficially rather than thoroughly. It is also challenging to distinguish between useful information and noise, and the abundance of options can make it difficult to select the most reliable or beneficial sources. This complicates the process of conducting thorough and high-quality research for students, as they may encounter difficulties in organising disparate pieces of information, identifying concealed biases, or comprehending intricate subjects. As an alternative, they may simply seek the most straightforward and expeditious solutions.

In this context, it is crucial to instruct students on how to assess sources and identify bias. It is no longer sufficient to provide students with information; they must be instructed on how to evaluate the legitimacy, reliability, and potential biases of online sources critically. This entails instructing children to verify the author's qualifications, analyse the publication dates, consider the domain (.org,.com,.gov), cross-reference the material with multiple reputable sources, and identify persuasive or emotive language. Students who lack these abilities are more susceptible to the effects of confirmation bias, propaganda, and deceptive information, particularly when they are presented with news that aligns with their preexisting beliefs on algorithmically designed social media platforms. The objective is to transition from passively consuming information to actively and critically engaging with the vast quantity of digital information that is available.

The Results of The Study: Teachers' Perceptions of Students' Communication Skills

Teachers in Idukki provided us with compelling firsthand accounts of their concerns regarding their students' communication skills in the digital era. Teachers' classroom challenges were effectively illustrated by these qualitative insights.

This was not a one-time issue; it was a prevalent issue in numerous regions. Teachers frequently addressed the issue of "wrong spellings in answer papers during exams." Teachers provided more specific examples of these "wrong spellings," typically referencing the use of text talk abbreviations in formal situations, such as writing "u" instead of "you," "bcoz" instead of "because," or omitting vowels in nouns. Additionally, they stated that the capitalisation and punctuation were generally subpar, with sentences occasionally running together without sufficient pauses or lacking any capital letters at the beginning of sentences. The teachers indicated that these errors were the result of "the after-effects of artificial intelligence, which is the auto-correction option while typing the text in social media chats." This indicates that they believed there was a strong correlation between digital habits and a decline in fundamental literacy.

Teachers also discussed the decline in the speaking abilities of children, in addition to writing. They observed that pupils appeared to be less confident or fluent when they were required to discuss complex concepts in person. This manifested as apprehension, the use of plain language, or difficulty initiating and maintaining a conversation. One educator may assert that a student is adept at conversing in online group chats but struggles to communicate plainly and confidently during a classroom presentation. This leads me to believe that the absence of real-time, unassisted communication with peers and the ability to compose remarks online may have an impact on students' confidence and proficiency in direct communication. The instructors' concerns regarding the "wrong spellings" issue prompted them to examine the function of auto-correction more closely. Auto-correction expedites digital messaging; however, it also facilitates accurate spelling. The minds of students are not actively engaged in the process of identifying and rectifying errors when they utilise this tool frequently. This can impede the brain's ability to develop a robust internal lexicon, which is the foundation of intrinsic spelling knowledge. Pupils may find it more challenging to spell as a result, as they become less adept at identifying their own errors and dependent on external technology support. In the long term, this will impede their capacity to write effectively and confidently without digital assistance, illustrating how an apparent innocuous technological convenience can gradually erode a fundamental academic skill.

Part 5: The Future of Human Connection: Beyond a Screen

In our Idukki research, we have meticulously examined the interaction between social media and face-to-face communication, as well as the disparities in the experiences of students and teachers. We have now reached the conclusion of our book. "The Future of Human Connection: Beyond the Screen" broadens the discourse by encouraging us to consider the broader implications of our digital advancements on society as a whole and offering a glimmer of hope for how individuals can not only endure but also flourish in an increasingly diverse world. This section summarises the critical points and anticipates the manner in which we will maintain communication in the digital era. We commence by discussing the concept of digital citizenship, acknowledging that social media can be either beneficial or detrimental. This section discusses the potential of social media to positively impact society and its members, with a particular emphasis on the necessity of fostering collaboration in order to effect change. This is exemplified by the Kerala Floods Relief Efforts, in which digital networks served as lifelines for the coordination and provision of humanitarian assistance. We will examine the increasing significance of citizen journalism in the reporting of news and the dissemination of awareness, as well as discuss specific examples of digital humanitarianism. However, we will also discuss the challenges associated with digital activism in a critical manner, including the concepts of "slacktivism" and the necessity for online activism to have tangible consequences. This section will also discuss the challenges of navigating echo chambers and polarisation in online discussions. It will elucidate how algorithmic filter chambers increase the likelihood of individuals adhering to their beliefs and how group polarisation can lead to individuals expressing more extreme opinions. It will also discuss strategies for fostering more civil and inclusive online discourse.

Next, we address the critical issue of the illusion of privacy, which renders our lives appear to be open journals online. We will discuss the concept of "surveillance capitalism," which refers to the method by which internet companies collect and sell user data, as well as the prevalent concerns regarding data privacy. We will discuss the "free" service paradox, in which consumers unknowingly pay with their information, and provide examples of large data breaches and their significant impacts on individuals. This section also discusses the "two faces" phenomenon, which is characterised by the distinction between curated online personas and real-life individuals. It discusses the emotional toll that inauthenticity imposes on the mental health of young adults, the emotional labour required to present an idealised self, and the impact it has on their self-esteem and identity formation. Most importantly, we will provide you with practical advice on how to establish boundaries in order to safeguard the digital identity. These will encompass fundamental digital hygiene recommendations, guidance on the comprehension and utilisation of privacy settings, and an examination of emerging legal frameworks such as "data portability" and "right to be forgotten."

Next, we examine methods for regaining presence through a mindful digital lifestyle as we progress towards solutions. This entails acknowledging the increasing prevalence of the digital detox, discussing its scientific advantages in terms of brain function, stress levels, and creativity, and discussing a variety of methods for implementing it, such as establishing daily restrictions and taking extended breaks. It also entails being forthright about the challenges and the potential for relapses. We will underscore the significance of cultivating empathy and active listening in a world that is rife with distractions. We will discuss the effectiveness of non-verbal feedback in face-to-face interactions, mindfulness techniques for communication, and educational methods such as communication workshops and role-playing. Additionally, this section will address the topic of maintaining a healthy balance between online and offline activities. Some suggestions include the implementation of "tech-free zones" and "time blocks" in daily life, the utilisation of technology to restrict screen time through app blockers and trackers, and the promotion of offline pursuits and activities to promote holistic development. Finally, this section discusses the manner in which individuals are evolving and the manner in which we are adjusting to a world that is both physical and digital. We will discuss the future of work and school, examining the increasing prevalence of blended realities and distant connections. We will also discuss hybrid work models and the challenges associated with establishing a team and culture when all employees work from home. We will also discuss the ongoing "digital divide" in hybrid learning and how having access to technology and a stable internet connection can result in unjust situations. We will discuss the importance of explicit communication in digital text, the development of "virtual presence," and the ability to read between the lines during video conversations. The section concludes by emphasising the significance of the "art of switching modes"—the capacity to seamlessly transition between digital and direct communication. The article also discusses the cognitive flexibility and intentionality that are essential for making the best communication choices, as well as the critical skill of practicing digital disengagement to be truly present in the moment. In a world that is increasingly digital, this comprehensive summary of the book's findings examines the ways in which individuals continue to establish connections with one another. It concludes with a plea for individuals to exercise greater caution in their utilisation of technology in order to enhance our humanity, rather than diminishing it.

Chapter 16: The Digital Citizen: Activism, Morality, and Duty on the Internet

The internet has evolved into a powerful platform for civic engagement, social commentary, and collective action, in addition to serving as a platform for social interaction and entertainment. It is crucial for both students and individuals to comprehend the moral implications and obligations that are associated with this environment. This chapter examines the potential of social media to serve as a potent force for good by uniting individuals to address a variety of issues, ranging from local concerns to global movements. It also examines the challenges associated with online discussions that are frequently polarised and echo chambers. Utilising social media for positive purposes: Engaging individuals in collaborative efforts to effect change, such as the relief efforts for the Kerala floods.

Social media is a highly effective instrument for social good that has the potential to unite individuals and resources at an unprecedented pace and scale. It provides individuals with a means to disseminate critical information, increase awareness, and organise relief efforts during disasters. The response to the devastating Kerala floods is a prime illustration of this transformative force, and it is particularly relevant to the region we examined. Social media served as an indispensable lifeline amid Kerala's catastrophic floods. When traditional forms of communication, such as television and telephones, were rendered unavailable due to power disruptions and infrastructure damage, platforms such as WhatsApp, Facebook, and X (formerly known as Twitter) emerged as the primary means of communication. Individuals who were impacted by the floods utilised these platforms to exchange instant messages, videos, and photographs, soliciting assistance and informing others of their whereabouts. Social media was employed by both celebrities and ordinary individuals to raise funds for relief operations and to disseminate information about them. The organisation of rescue efforts and the distribution of relief were facilitated by the ability of individuals to independently locate and join volunteer groups through digital networks. In numerous instances, individuals from other sites offered their assistance with rescue operations through the use of social media. This decentralised, real-time coordination was instrumental in securing financial and humanitarian assistance from a variety of global entities.

In addition to disaster response, there are numerous specific examples of digital humanitarianism in which social media played a significant role in the pursuit of social welfare. Worldwide, platforms have been implemented to organise blood donation campaigns, raise funds for medical emergencies, assist in the search for missing individuals, and organise environmental protection initiatives. For instance, social media facilitated the communication between individuals who were stranded and rescuers during the floods in Chennai, as well as the dissemination of information regarding relief shelters, similar to the situation in Kerala. The effectiveness of campaigns for animal welfare, food distribution for the impoverished, and educational programs for impoverished children has been significantly enhanced by digital networks. This demonstrates that social media has the potential to transform online awareness into tangible assistance and encouragement.

The function of citizen journalism is closely associated with this event. In an era in which traditional media outlets may lack the necessary resources or are unable to access specific regions, ordinary individuals with cell phones have emerged as effective reporters. They frequently provide individuals on the ground with immediate, unedited news by utilising social media to film events as they occur, acquire unadulterated footage, and publish first-hand accounts. During protests, natural disasters, or periods of injustice, citizen journalists can bypass conventional gatekeepers and provide a global audience with critical information and perspectives. This democratisation of news reporting empowers individuals to contribute to public discourse, hold authorities accountable, and raise awareness of local issues, thereby altering the manner in which information is disseminated.

Conversely, it is crucial to address the challenges associated with digital activism, which some individuals refer to as "slacktivism." This term denotes online actions such as signing a petition or sharing a post that require minimal effort and are occasionally perceived as lacking in real-world impact or genuine commitment. Despite the fact that these actions do raise awareness, some individuals argue that they may not result in the long-term effort or real-world participation necessary for systemic change. Social media has the potential to initiate and expand movements; however, genuine social change often necessitates individuals to take organised, long-term, and frequently difficult action in the real world, rather than simply clicking a button. This criticism demonstrates that internet activism should be a means to engage individuals more deeply, rather than merely a means to compel them to act.

The Power of Collaboration: From Local Issues to Global Movements

In addition to aiding in the aftermath of disasters, social media can also facilitate collaboration among individuals to address a diverse array of social and political issues. It has increased the accessibility of activism, enabling individuals to participate in movements, express their opinions, and alter the manner in which people discuss topics in a manner that was previously only feasible for traditional media or organised political groups.

Social media has been a powerful force for change, as demonstrated by numerous case studies of social justice movements. For instance, the #MeToo movement gained unprecedented global momentum through social media, enabling survivors of sexual harassment and assault to share their narratives, demand accountability, and receive support. In the same vein, climate strikes organised by youth activists were able to garner worldwide support through internet coordination, resulting in millions of young people from around the world calling for immediate action on climate change. Social media has been employed by Black Lives Matter and other regional demonstrations against injustice to rapidly disseminate information, organise protests, and communicate their messages to a global audience. This demonstrates the potency of social media in uniting individuals in support of shared causes.

This mobilisation is centred around the utilisation of viral content and hashtags. Hashtags such as #KeralaFloods, #MeToo, and #ClimateStrike are effective for organising conversations because they facilitate the identification of pertinent content and the participation in group discussions by bringing together individuals who are discussing a variety of topics. Content can become "viral," which refers to its rapid dissemination through shares, retweets, and likes, regardless of whether it is a captivating image, a poignant film, or a concise message. This viral mechanism enables messages to reach millions of individuals in a brief period of time, bypassing conventional gatekeepers. This enables the direct transmission of accounts from grassroots organisations or communities that have been impacted. This rapid dissemination of information and emotional connection enables individuals to rapidly mobilise and become aware on a large scale.

It is crucial to recognise that social media platforms are not exclusively intended for online discourse. In addition, they are increasingly employed to plan and coordinate actions in the real world. In the actual world, activists employ these sites to organise and execute protests, rallies, and community events. For example, a neighbourhood organisation may recruit volunteers for a clean-up through a WhatsApp group, or a Facebook event could disseminate information about a public meeting regarding a local issue. It is effortless to deliberate on intricate logistics, safety, and meeting locations. This seamless transition from online discourse to in-person engagement demonstrates the potential of digital tools to facilitate community engagement in the real world, transforming online solidarity into tangible action.

How to Navigate Polarisation and Echo Chambers in Online Conversations

Social media has the potential to facilitate collaboration and democratic engagement among individuals; however, it also presents numerous challenges, including the proliferation of echo chambers and the escalation of polarisation. The algorithms that are intended to enhance the personalisation of our online experiences may inadvertently generate digital chambers in which individuals are only presented with information and opinions that align with their preexisting beliefs.

This is elucidated by algorithmic filter bubbles. In order to maintain people's interest, social media algorithms present them with content that they are most likely to engage with. This implies that the algorithm will selectively exclude other viewpoints or points of view while displaying an increased amount of content that aligns with a particular political stance to an individual who frequently interacts with it. This results in the user being trapped in a "filter bubble," where they are primarily presented with information that supports their preexisting beliefs. This can result in individuals having a distorted perception of reality, which leads them to believe that their perspective is more prevalent than it actually is and that opinions that differ from their own are uncommon or preposterous.

In these filter chambers, the psychology of group polarisation is established. People's original notions tend to become more extreme when they primarily converse with individuals who share their perspective online. People in these groups frequently discuss their shared beliefs, which results in a stronger sense of attachment to them and a reduced capacity to think critically about themselves. This can result in a perilous lack of critical engagement with alternative perspectives, which can make it difficult to engage in productive conversations or establish common ground with individuals who do not share the perspective. Additionally, individuals may experience greater autonomy in expressing more extreme or aggressive sentiments online due to the uncertainty surrounding their identity and the distance between them. This exacerbates the polarisation.

In order to address these issues, it is imperative that we implement measures to promote civil discourse. This entails the encouragement of media literacy courses that instruct children on how to identify algorithmic biases and seek alternative perspectives. Structured debates or moderated forums that encourage respectful online discourse are examples of initiatives that can facilitate the unification of individuals. Additionally, individuals may engage in conscious information assimilation by adhering to a variety of news sources and viewpoints, including those with which they disagree, in order to acquire additional knowledge. Additionally, educating individuals on how to think critically and empathise may facilitate their engagement with online content in a more contemplative manner, enabling them to develop a more profound understanding of complex subjects and recognise the individual behind the computer. Social media not only connects us, but it also increases our awareness of these inherent biases and compels us to actively seek out alternative perspectives in order to avoid becoming ensnared in a cycle of digital division and confirmation bias.

Chapter 17: The Illusion of Privacy: Our Lives Are Like Open Books

The digital era has brought about significant changes in the realm of privacy. The concept of personal space and private information, which was once straightforward, has evolved into a complex and frequently ambiguous landscape. Social media platforms are beneficial for maintaining communication and simplifying tasks; however, their commercial model contradicts conventional notions of privacy, rendering our lives transparent. This chapter discusses the prevalent concerns regarding data privacy, the "two faces" phenomenon, in which controlled online personas differ from real-life selves, and provides practical advice for establishing boundaries to ensure the safety of one's digital self in a world that is becoming increasingly transparent.

Who is the proprietor of the information? These concerns pertain to privacy.

In the era of social media, the most significant threats to privacy are data ownership and control. By creating a social media account, we frequently grant the platforms significant authority to collect, analyse, and potentially sell our personal information without our knowledge. A huge, intricate profile of our likes, dislikes, behaviours, interests, and even our moods is constructed with each click, post, "like," search query, and interaction. This data is frequently referred to as the "new oil," and it is of considerable value.

Shoshana Zuboff, a scholar, refers to this widespread data collection as "Surveillance Capitalism." In this economic system, personal data is transformed into a commodity, and tech companies secretly collect vast quantities of behavioural data from users, predict their future actions, and subsequently sell these predictions to advertisers and other businesses. It is a form of capitalism that generates revenue not only through the sale of goods and services, but also through the meticulous observation of human behaviour. This implies that, despite the perception that social media is free, users are essentially the raw material that is being processed and sold. This fundamental economic concept is essential for comprehending the difficulty of safeguarding privacy in the digital age.

This is the reason the "free" service paradox is so peculiar: the notion that the consumer is not the product, but rather the service when it is "free." Users are not required to pay explicitly for the services that social media platforms provide. However, their substantial revenues and value are derived from their capacity to gather, analyse, and utilise user data to create advertisements that are highly pertinent to each individual. By forfeiting their confidential information, time, and behavioural insights, users "pay" for the convenience of connecting and obtaining content. This implicit trade may be overlooked or misunderstood by users, particularly those who are young. They may be unaware of the extent to which their digital lives are being monitored and merchandised.

The consequences of amassing an excessive amount of data are not merely hypothetical; they manifest in the real world, particularly when data is taken and the subsequent events occur. Even with the most stringent security measures, no system is entirely secure. The private information of millions of individuals is at risk as a result of the increasing frequency of major data intrusions. For instance, the Cambridge Analytica incident demonstrated the unauthorised use of Facebook users' confidential information to create political advertisements. Other breaches have disclosed financial information, phone numbers, email addresses, and even names, increasing the likelihood of identity theft, phishing schemes, and online harassment. The repercussions on individuals can be severe, encompassing financial losses, reputational damage, mental distress, and feelings of privacy invasion. These occurrences serve as a stark reminder that the illusion of anonymity that is prevalent online can be easily compromised, exposing individuals to unforeseen challenges.

Real Life vs. Curated Online Life: The "Two Faces" Phenomenon

Chapter 7 discusses the "two faces" phenomenon, which is the result of the desire to present an idealised version of oneself on social media. This implies that the meticulously constructed, frequently flawless online identity is becoming increasingly distinct from the more intricate, real, and occasionally chaotic offline existence.

These consistent performances have significant psychological consequences due to their lack of authenticity. When individuals consistently exhibit an idealised version of themselves that does not align with their true emotions or experiences, it can result in a sense of emotional dissonance and inauthenticity. This can manifest as anxiety due to their perpetual concern about maintaining the façade, or as a sense of being estranged from their authentic selves. Maintaining this controlled persona can be emotionally taxing, resulting in a diminished sense of self-worth and mental fatigue that arise from seeking approbation from others rather than expressing happiness with oneself. Internal conflict and a diminished sense of self-acceptance are more probable when this distinction is more apparent.

This is a result of the desire to achieve success. Social media platforms are analogous to stages, where individuals consistently perform for their peers. People are motivated to showcase only the most desirable, fascinating, and best aspects of their lives in order to attract a large number of followers, "likes," and positive comments. It may be challenging to maintain the emotional investment that is required to select the appropriate photo, compose a humorous post, and oversee one's online presence. Rather than being genuinely lived and cherished for their own sake, it transforms everyday life into a series of potential photo ops or shareable moments. Individuals who are perpetually engaged in performance may only be superficially engaged in life, valuing events more for their ease of communication than for their true significance.

This distinction between the online and offline persona has a significant impact on the development of self-esteem and identity, particularly among young adults. It is crucial for adolescents and young adults to establish a robust sense of self during this critical period of their lives. Students' self-esteem may be negatively impacted, and they may feel inadequate when they consistently contrast their imperfect lives with the flawless highlight reels of their peers and influencers. Individuals who seek validation online may develop an unhealthy dependence on it to enhance their self-esteem, rendering them susceptible to other individuals' approval. This may complicate the process of young adults developing a healthy sense of self, as they may struggle to discern the distinction between their authentic selves and the idealised version of themselves, they believe they are required to present online. This can result in them becoming perplexed about their genuine identity.

Establishing Boundaries: Strategies for Protecting the Digital Identity

Consciously establishing boundaries is a critical measure for safeguarding one's digital identity and maintaining a positive relationship with technology in an era in which privacy is becoming increasingly difficult to attain and the distinctions between online and offline are becoming increasingly unclear. This entails making deliberate decisions and aggressively taking action to regain control over the digital footprint and personal space.

First and foremost, it is crucial to adhere to proper digital hygiene protocols. This entails the use of robust, distinctive passwords for all of the online accounts and the activation of two-factor authentication (2FA) whenever feasible. This provides an additional element of security. It is also crucial to remain vigilant for phishing attempts, which are fraudulent emails or messages that attempt to deceive individuals into disclosing sensitive information. It is also crucial to be aware of the potential hazards associated with public Wi-Fi networks, as they may not be secure. Additionally, it is crucial to avoid transmitting sensitive information over unencrypted channels. These fundamental precautions significantly reduce the likelihood of an individual gaining access to the personal information without the consent.

Secondly, it is crucial to take the initiative to become familiar with and implement privacy settings on all social media platforms. Users have the ability to limit the visibility of their posts, the ability to contact them, the ability to identify them in photographs, and the data that is collected and shared with third parties. These options are frequently difficult to locate and are concealed in the menus. Rather than relying on the default options, it is possible to exert greater control over the digital presence by consistently reviewing and modifying these settings. For instance, restricting the audience to "friends" rather than "public" may significantly restrict their visibility. Another critical measure in safeguarding the privacy is to be aware of the permissions that applications possess and to remove them from applications that no longer require them.

Finally, it is imperative that individuals are apprised of the latest legal and ethical regulations regarding the ownership and management of data, including the right to be forgotten and data portability. In certain jurisdictions, the "right to be forgotten" allows individuals to request that search engines remove hyperlinks to outdated or irrelevant personal information. "Data portability" refers to the ability to obtain the personal data in a structured, machine-readable format that is widely used and can be transferred to another service provider. Although these rights are still evolving globally, the knowledge of them enables individuals to advocate for greater autonomy over their digital identities and to demand that technology corporations be more transparent and forthright in their data usage. By actively establishing these boundaries and engaging with new privacy frameworks, individuals can transition from passive consumers of digital content to empowered architects of their own digital lives. This will assist them in safeguarding their privacy, mental health, and the authenticity of their true selves in a world that is increasingly transparent.

Chapter 18: Taking Back Presence: Tips for Living Mindfully in the Digital Age.

In a world replete with digital distractions, the screen relentlessly tugs at our attention, the capacity to be fully present—completely engaged in the present moment—has become exceedingly rare. Technology simplifies tasks and establishes connections that were previously unattainable; however, it also complicates the process of maintaining focus, forging genuine relationships with others, and locating tranquilly amid the perpetual digital cacophony. This chapter transitions from analysis to action, exploring practical methods for reconnecting with the present through mindful digital living. It addresses the increasing prevalence of digital detoxification and the cultivation of critical competencies such as active listening and empathy. Additionally, it provides specific instructions for achieving a harmonious equilibrium between an active online presence and a fulfilling offline existence.

The Digital Detox Trend: Disconnecting from Technology to Connect

The "digital detox" is one of the simplest and increasingly popular methods for reconnecting with the present. It involves consciously refraining from using digital devices and social media for a designated period, which may range from a few hours to a few days or even weeks. The rationale for this trend is straightforward: to re-establish a connection with the real world, other individuals, and oneself by ceasing the constant mental noise, scrolling, and monitoring that digital platforms may induce.

The increasing prevalence of digital detoxes is supported by new scientific evidence. Research indicates that a vacation from digital devices can be beneficial for the brain, as it reduces cognitive overload and facilitates concentration. Studies have demonstrated that even brief periods of non-technology use can reduce tension levels, as individuals are relieved of the constant burden of social comparison and notifications. Digital detoxes have also been associated with an increase in creativity, as they provide the mind with the opportunity to explore and consider in novel ways without constant external stimulation. An additional prevalent benefit is improved sleep. Melatonin production is facilitated by reducing screen time prior to bedtime. These scientific discoveries demonstrate that intentionally disconnecting is not merely a trend, but a viable approach to enhancing one's emotional and mental well-being.

Numerous methods exist for conducting a digital detox, allowing individuals to select the method that is most conducive to their well-being and preferences. Some individuals opt to establish daily boundaries, which may involve refraining from using any digital devices that are not essential during specific hours in the morning or evening. Some individuals prefer to take breaks on the weekends and spend the entire Saturday or Sunday offline, engaging in pastimes, spending time with family and friends, or being in nature. Some individuals engage in extended detoxification excursions or personal retreats, during which they refrain from using screens for a period of one week or more. This is a more profound reset. The most critical factors are to be intentional and consistent, as well as to select a method that is suitable for the needs and provides a genuine respite from constant online activity.

However, initiating a digital detox is not an effortless endeavour, and there is a possibility of relapsing. Social media has powerful psychological incentive loops, which can make it difficult to break profoundly ingrained digital habits. Individuals may experience feelings of anxiety, restlessness, or an overwhelming desire to constantly inspect their devices upon ceasing their use. Fear of missing out (FOMO) can also be a significant issue that makes it difficult to resist the allure of online notifications. It may also be challenging to maintain a long-term disconnect when the peers are perpetually active on social media. It is crucial to be aware of these issues in order to establish achievable objectives and devise strategies for overcoming them. This may involve informing friends and family members of the intentions so that they can help.

How to Foster Empathy and Active Listening in a World Overrun by Distractions

The constant interruption of our attention by digital distractions significantly hinders our ability to truly attend to and comprehend others. In a world where a signal can swiftly divert our attention, the cultivation of active listening and empathy necessitates effort and repetition. Active listening is not merely the act of hearing words; it involves paying close attention to the speaker's message, both audibly and non-verbally, determining its significance, and responding in a deliberate manner.

Active listening can be enhanced through the use of mindfulness techniques in communication. Mindful breathing, which involves taking a few deep breaths to quiet the thoughts and concentrate on the present, is a straightforward method to mute internal distractions before you begin speaking. By remaining cognisant of the thoughts and emotions without passing judgement on them during the conversation, you can concentrate more on the other individual's perspective. This intentional endeavour to be fully engaged in the conversation enables individuals to resist the inclination to contemplate their own responses during the other person's speech, thereby dedicating their mental energy to comprehending the message.

It is crucial to comprehend the potential impact of nonverbal feedback. Our bodies and expressions communicate as much, if not more, than our words when we converse with someone in person. In order to consciously comprehend and utilise nonverbal cues, it is necessary to maintain eye contact (without gazing), occasionally nod to indicate comprehension, maintain an open and responsive body, and imitate minor movements to establish rapport. It is equally important to comprehend how to interpret these signals from others. For instance, a stiff posture may indicate discomfort, a furrowed brow may indicate perplexity, and a faint smile may indicate something else. By attending to these unspoken signals, individuals can engage in more intricate and compassionate conversations. This enables them to comprehend the emotional undertones of a conversation.

Role-playing and communication seminars can be extremely beneficial methods for improving one's listening skills, in addition to independent practice. In a secure, regulated environment, participants can hone their active listening abilities, receive feedback on their body language, and engage in simulated difficult conversations. These sessions can assist students, such as those in our Idukki study, in developing a greater sense of confidence in their ability to engage in lengthy, meaningful conversations in person. Schools may be able to halt the decline of direct communication skills in a world that is replete with technology by explicitly teaching and exercising these interpersonal skills. This will produce a generation that is proficient in both technology and interpersonal communication.

How to Maintain a Healthy Balance Between the Online and Offline Lives in Real Life

The objective is not to eliminate technology; rather, it is to prudently integrate it into our daily lives in order to achieve a harmonious equilibrium between online and offline life. It implements deliberate measures that prioritise personal health and real-world interactions. These are several practical actions that are accessible to all individuals, particularly students:

Establishing "Tech-Free Zones" and "Time Blocks": This entails the deliberate removal of digital devices from specific locations and during specific times. For example, during family dinners, the dining room table can be designated as a "no-phone zone" to encourage conversation. Establishing "tech-free time blocks," such as the first hour after waking up, the last hour before bed, or specific study periods, may also assist in regaining the attention and personal time. Students may opt to maintain a technology-free bedroom for non-academic purposes, as this would facilitate their ability to sleep and unwind.

Limiting technology through technology: It is amusing, but technology can actually assist in the regulation of one's digital behaviours. App blockers can be employed by students to disable social media applications that are disruptive during study sessions. Typically, screen time monitors are integrated into smartphones to provide users with information regarding the amount of time they spend on their devices each day. This increases their awareness and enables them to establish realistic boundaries. Users are able to select which applications are permitted to send them alerts through notification management tools, which reduces the frequency of interruptions. Intentionally altering these settings allows individuals to regain control of their devices, rather than allowing them to dominate them.

Promoting Hobbies and Activities That Do Not Involve Screens: It is essential to actively pursue and engage in hobbies and activities that do not involve screens in order to achieve a harmonious balance between one's online and offline existence. You may engage in a variety of activities, such as participating in a sports team, learning to perform an instrument, creating art or writing, contributing to the community, or simply spending time outdoors in nature. By promoting participation in these non-screen activities, individuals are provided with enjoyable activities to engage in, which reduces their time spent on screens, aids in the acquisition of new knowledge, expands their social networks in the real world, and fosters personal development.

This could also entail students rediscovering the pleasure of perusing genuine books, engaging in board games with friends, or simply conversing with one another without the use of a device.
By adhering to these straightforward procedures, individuals can cease passively consuming digital content and begin actively influencing their own digital well-being. This strategy is designed to enable individuals to take advantage of the advantages of being online while also regaining the priceless profundity of genuine, present, and sincere offline human connection. This results in a more balanced and fulfilled life.

Chapter 19: The Evolving Human: Strategies for Existing in a Hybrid World

The manner in which individuals interact with one another has been significantly altered by the digital revolution. It has established a hybrid society in which the real and virtual realms are perpetually intertwined. This novel approach necessitates that we consistently adjust. In order to thrive in environments where online and offline components are interwoven, it is necessary to modify our social norms, perspectives, and capabilities. The future of employment and school in these mixed realities is the subject of this chapter. It also discusses the importance of the "art of switching modes," which is the capacity to effortlessly transition between digital and face-to-face communication, as well as the emergence of new forms of emotional intelligence that are particularly relevant in virtual environments.

The Future of Work and School: Balancing Realities and Working from Home

Digital connectivity has revolutionised the manner in which we learn and work, rendering it impossible to revert to the previous state. This transformation occurred at an accelerated pace as a result of recent global events that necessitated remote work and online education. These occurrences

demonstrated that hybrid realities are feasible and, in numerous instances, function effectively. In the future, it will be more prevalent in both professional and academic settings to employ a hybrid approach that integrates the most advantageous aspects of both.
This implies that hybrid work models will become increasingly prevalent in the workplace. One such example is the "3-2-2 model," which involves employees working collaboratively in the office for three days, working remotely for two days, and taking two days off. In certain models, employees are only required to attend specific team meetings or customer presentations inside the office. The majority of their labour is conducted from home. Companies are structuring their operations to enable them to utilise digital tools for routine tasks and reserve their physical offices for activities that are most effectively conducted in person, such as ideation, mentoring, and socialising. This adaptability offers advantages such as a greater reservoir of talent to select from, a more favourable work-life balance, and shorter commutes. Nevertheless, it also necessitates the development of novel methods for communication and collaboration.

However, the development and maintenance of a culture with remote teams are impeded by these muddled realities. When teams are dispersed, it can be challenging to ensure that all members agree, establish a robust company culture, and ensure that everyone feels a sense of belonging. Individuals are less inclined to engage in spontaneous conversations that foster the development of novel concepts or the strengthening of relationships. Companies must actively invest in virtual team-building activities, regular check-ins, and explicit communication norms to ensure that remote workers feel connected and valued. In order to effectively manage distributed teams, leadership approaches must be modified to prioritise results over mere presence. The objective is to prevent individuals from experiencing feelings of isolation or disconnection when the majority of their interactions occur through displays.

Similarly, the transition to hybrid learning models in education presents its own set of challenges, particularly in terms of the "digital divide" in hybrid learning. Despite the fact that online components provide individuals with a plethora of information and more options, they can also exacerbate inequalities. Students from low-income households may not have consistent access to high-speed internet, the appropriate equipment (such as laptops instead of shared smartphones), or a tranquil home environment that is conducive to online learning. This creates a "digital divide," in which certain children are more effective in hybrid settings than others, potentially exacerbating achievement disparities. In order to resolve this issue, educational institutions must implement measures to ensure that all students, irrespective of their background or location, have equitable access to technology, internet subsidies, and assistance with digital literacy. This will ensure that integrated learning models are accessible to all individuals.

New Skills for a New Time: Emotional Intelligence in Virtual Settings

Traditionally, emotional intelligence was defined as the capacity to perceive, understand, regulate, and employ emotions when engaging in interpersonal communication. However, the situation becomes more intricate in virtual environments. Text-based communication is devoid of critical nonverbal signals, and video calls are occasionally interrupted or delayed. This implies that individuals must acquire new abilities in order to effectively communicate and interpret emotions online. The term "digital emotional intelligence" was first introduced at this time. One critical skill for this era is the ability to establish a "virtual presence," which entails the ability to convey authenticity, charisma, and engagement through a screen. It is imperative that individuals intentionally enhance their verbal and visual communication skills, as subtle nonverbal indicators are less apparent. This could entail maintaining eye contact with the camera to simulate that you are gazing at the other individual, employing expressive facial gestures, altering the tone and pitch of the voice to convey emotion, and ensuring that the illumination is appropriate and the background is professional. In virtual meetings, it is more crucial to demonstrate the engagement by speaking affirmations (such as "I understand" or "That makes sense"), asking questions, and actively participating. This compensates for the absence of immediate physical input.

Additionally, individuals must enhance their ability to interpret signals during video calls, particularly when the quality of the image is subpar. It necessitates a greater degree of concentration to comprehend micro expressions, minute posture adjustments, or fleeting glances at a two-dimensional screen. Even if you are unable to observe all of the body language, observing head gestures, hand movements, and facial expressions (even if they are pixelated) can still provide you with valuable information about the other person's emotions or level of interest. This also entails exercising caution in the manner in which you exhibit the self-online, ensuring that the nonverbal cues are consistent with the verbal communication to prevent individuals from forming an inaccurate impression.

Explicit communication is more critical than ever in digital communication, potentially even more so than in person. In the absence of numerous or any nonverbal signals, individuals must be more explicit about their emotions and intentions through digital text or speech. In order to prevent misunderstandings, it is necessary to either explain out or display subtle emotions, humour, or sarcasm that would be easily comprehensible in person. A smiley face or the phrase "OK, sounds good!" can be incorporated into a basic "OK" to indicate that you are sincere. In the workplace, this entails the use of unambiguous language, the avoidance of confusion, and the request for clarification when one is uncertain about the meaning or tone of a message. Opening up about one's emotions and objectives intentionally facilitates the closure of the emotional divide that is inherent in digital interactions, thereby fostering a more profound connection and comprehension.

The Art of Mode Switching: Transitioning from Digital to Direct Without a Hitch

The "art of switching modes" is likely the most critical skill for managing the evolving human experience. This entails the ability to seamlessly transition between digital and direct modes of communication. It is not a matter of selecting one over the other; rather, it is a matter of recognising the optimal time to switch between each phase and seamlessly transitioning between them to optimise their effectiveness.

In order to master this discipline, it is essential to be highly adaptable and cognisant of the circumstances. Cognitive flexibility is the capacity to adjust one's thoughts and behaviours to accommodate novel, evolving, or unexpected circumstances. This entails the ability to promptly adjust the communication style, vocabulary, and expectations in accordance with the channel you are utilising (e.g., a formal email, a casual WhatsApp conversation, or an in-person meeting). In order to be context-aware, it is necessary to be aware of the social norms, expectations, and boundaries of any communication environment. For instance, a high level of context awareness is demonstrated by the recognition that a face-to-face conversation is optimal for a complex emotional subject, and a text message is the most effective for a brief factual update. People are able to select the most effective, efficient, and emotionally resonant method of communication with others due to this mental flexibility.

This leads to the concept of intentionality in the decisions we make regarding our communication style. It is not sufficient for individuals to utilise the most expeditious or convenient channel; rather, they should consider the appropriate channel for the specific message. For example, a student may utilise a WhatsApp group to schedule a study session (efficiency) but subsequently consult with their teacher in person to obtain a more detailed and nuanced explanation of a complex concept (depth and subtlety). A professional may elect to utilise a video conference for a sensitive feedback session, despite the fact that they may send out formal announcements via email. This level of consideration ensures that the channel of communication is appropriate for the emotional weight and objective of the message, thereby minimising the likelihood of misunderstandings and maximising its effectiveness.

Finally, a critical component of this discipline is the practice of digital disengagement, which entails putting one's phone aside and being fully engaged in the present moment. This entails actively resisting the inclination to check alerts while engaging in in-person activities such as dining, conversing, or engaging in other activities. It suggests the capacity to "detach" one's consciousness from the digital realm and concentrate solely on the individuals and objects in the physical world. This skill is crucial for the development of active listening, genuine empathy, and the ability to engage in face-to-face interactions without being distracted by digital devices. People who possess the ability to transition between modes can effortlessly navigate the hybrid environment, utilising technology to its maximum potential while simultaneously fervently preserving and fostering the distinctive depth of direct, human connection.

Chapter 20: The Connected Paradox: Combining Our Knowledge and Urging Individuals to Act

After traversing the intricate realms of digital transformation, the subtleties of human connection, and the distinctive experiences of students and teachers in Idukki, we have arrived at a critical juncture: the integration of our discoveries to gain a comprehensive understanding of the "connected paradox." This chapter unites the threads of our investigation, emphasising the intricate relationship between social media and face-to-face communication, summarising the primary findings of our pioneering research, and ultimately encouraging individuals and society to be more deliberate and reflective in this hybrid environment.

Summing Up: The Interplay Between Face-to-Face Communication and social media

The central concept of this book is that social media and in-person communication are not merely two aspects of the same coin. Instead, they are perpetually evolving and engaging with one another in a manner that is occasionally advantageous and others challenging. Our research has demonstrated that the proliferation of digital connectivity does not imply that face-to-face interactions will be entirely replaced; rather, they will be fundamentally redefined and altered.

To clarify this connection, it is crucial to recognise that social media and in-person communication are not merely substituting one another; they are also interdependent. Social media is frequently employed by individuals to discuss matters prior to or following in-person meetings. Students may establish a study group via WhatsApp, which may result in an in-person meeting. After an event, individuals may continue to converse and share photographs online, thereby prolonging the social experience. This implies that internet platforms do not always prevent individuals from attending in person; rather, they may enhance the experience or help. The relationship is complex due to the fact that digital tools can sometimes impede profound human connection and at the same time be beneficial.

The most effective method of comprehending this intricate relationship is through the use of the double-edged weapon metaphor. Social media presents both substantial opportunities and significant challenges. It offers numerous advantages, including the facilitation of global communication, the establishment of connections across vast distances, the ability to collaborate during crises (as evidenced by the Kerala floods relief efforts), the provision of a plethora of educational resources, and the development of novel mechanisms for self-expression and community building. For many individuals, it is an indispensable method of maintaining communication with family and friends, receiving news, and following their interests. The other side of the sword, however, reveals its shortcomings: the stress of curated online personas, the subtle allure of distraction and procrastination, the loss of deep focus, the significant issues with personal privacy, and the minor impacts on our capacity to engage with others in a nuanced manner, such as the decrease in active listening and the increase in informal language in formal settings.

Additionally, the significance of context cannot be overstated when discussing the consequences of social media. The effects of digital engagement are not universal; they are contingent upon the individual, their culture, and the situation. The manner in which social media alters an individual's communication with others can be influenced by their disposition (introvert vs. extrovert), the social support networks they already have, their proficiency with technology, and their cultural heritage. For example, in societies that prioritise the group over the individual, the manner in which individuals communicate with one another in group conversations may differ significantly from their individual interactions. The age range of the users, the purpose for the communication (academic vs. social), and the platform used all have an equal impact. It is crucial to comprehend these subtle distinctions in context in order to avoid making generalised statements and to develop specific strategies for promoting healthy digital behaviours.

What We Discovered About Influence and Correlation from the Idukki Study

The real-world evidence we obtained from our extensive investigation in Idukki was instrumental in our comprehension of this intricate relationship. It provided us with comprehensive information regarding the interplay between social media usage and in-person communication among undergraduate students and professors.

The findings indicated that there was a statistically significant, moderate, and positive correlation between the use of social media and speaking with individuals in person. The p-value of 0.000 indicates that this discovery is quite robust and that the link is highly unlikely to be the result of coincidence. Although a moderate correlation implies that social media usage is not the sole factor predicting face-to-face communication, it does demonstrate a persistent connection. This implies that the two modes of communication are interconnected, and social media may serve as a facilitator or parallel path rather than a direct replacement. For example, pupils may utilise social media to maintain communication with a greater number of individuals, which either increases their desire to meet in person or provides them with additional opportunities to do so.

The qualitative information we obtained from our conversations with teachers provided us with a wealth of context and enabled us to employ more specific teacher anecdotes to elucidate our point. Numerous seasoned educators expressed concern that digital distractions were diminishing the significance of in-person interactions, as evidenced by statements such as, "Students are perpetually engaged with their phones, even when they are in close proximity. They are connected to the world, but occasionally less so." "I frequently observe incorrect spellings in examination papers," stated an additional educator. "It appears that they have become so dependent on WhatsApp's autocorrect feature that they have forgotten how to spell correctly independently." This example demonstrates their concern regarding the potential loss of fundamental reading and writing abilities in children. These narratives collectively demonstrate that educators are grappling with the unexpected consequences of students' digital behaviours on their academic performance and communication skills.

The results of our study have significant implications for policy and practice, particularly in the field of education. The significance of acting prior to a negative event is demonstrated by the link that was discovered and the concerns of educators. This implies that there should be explicit guidelines regarding the use of smartphones in the classroom for school policy. They are not required to be prohibited; however, they should be employed in a manner that is logical. In the context of digital literacy programs, this entails transitioning from the instruction of "how to use" technology to the instruction of "how to use it responsibly and critically." The primary emphasis of these programs should be on media literacy, digital decorum, and the importance of maintaining a balance between online and actual interactions. The findings suggest that schools should intentionally instruct students on the "art of switching modes," which involves the effective transition between digital and direct contact. They should also establish an environment that prioritises genuine connections with others and profound, concentrated learning.

A Fair Perspective: Recognising the Positive and Minimising the Negative

A balanced perspective is necessary to comprehend the connected paradox. It is neither logical nor beneficial to advocate for a complete prohibition of social media. Its advantages are undeniable, and it is an indispensable component of contemporary existence. However, in order to capitalise on these advantages, it is imperative to recognise the risks associated with them and implement measures to mitigate them.

The term "digital well-being" encapsulates this comprehensive approach. This broader concept extends beyond mere prevention of negative outcomes and instead promotes a productive, positive, and enjoyable relationship with technology. Digital well-being encompasses a variety of activities, such as regulating screen time, utilising technology sensibly, safeguarding privacy, fostering positive online relationships, and ensuring that technology enhances rather than detracts from mental and physical health. It is about empowering individuals to manage their technology, rather than allowing it to dictate their actions.

In order to achieve this digital well-being, it is imperative that all individuals assume responsibility for both them and society. Individuals must assume accountability for their digital behaviours by exercising self-control and being deliberate. Teachers play a critical role in the education of children on the safe use of technology, the development of critical thinking skills, and the responsibility associated with technology. It is imperative that parents collaborate with schools, establish boundaries at home, and instruct their children on the proper use of technology. It is also crucial for digital businesses to develop platforms that prioritise the health and safety of users, implement ethical data methods, and offer features that promote conscious use, rather than solely focussing on increasing user engagement. Lastly, it is imperative that legislators establish regulations that protect the privacy of individuals, address online issues such as cyberbullying and false information, and ensure that all individuals have equal access to digital resources.

Therefore, the findings of our Idukki study indicate that it is imperative that we adopt a proactive approach. In a world where technology is an integral component of our daily existence, it is impossible to continue passively consuming digital content and without regulating our screen time. Our mental health, communication, and overall well-being must be actively managed, and we must make a conscious effort to comprehend the impact of our tools on these areas. This entails transcending the mere act of being "connected" to being "mindfully connected," utilising technology to its full potential while simultaneously fervently preserving and promoting the distinctive profundity of direct, human connection that serves as the fundamental bedrock of our social structure. The key to success in our lives, which are becoming increasingly complex, is this balanced perspective.

Chapter 21: The Way Forward and the Unanswered Questions

It is evident that the digital revolution is a continuous narrative that is subject to change as a result of new technology, evolving societal norms, and unforeseen consequences as we conclude our examination of the linked paradox. Our research in Idukki has provided us with critical insights into the interplay between face-to-face communication and social media. Nevertheless, it has also left us with a multitude of unresolved issues and demonstrated the significance of continuing to pose questions. This final chapter examines the future and discusses critical areas that require further investigation. It also contemplates the perpetual evolution of technology and the potential frontiers of human interaction. Lastly, it provides a concluding reflection on the collective obligation to ensure that the digital future is a place that prioritises genuine human interaction.

Future Research Areas: Conducting long-term investigations and expanding beyond Idukki

Our research encompasses a wide range of topics and provides valuable insights from a particular rural Indian context; however, it is merely a moment in time and space. In order to gain a more comprehensive understanding of the connected paradox, it is imperative to investigate a number of critical areas for future research.

Initially, it is crucial to move beyond Idukki. Unique insights into a rural area that is also digitally advanced were provided by our district-specific focus. Nevertheless, it is necessary to conduct comparable research in various regions of India, including remote tribal areas and bustling metropolitan areas with their own digital cultures, where internet access may still be restricted. This would enable us to gain a more comprehensive understanding of the impact of social media on individuals in relation to their economic circumstances, cultural norms, and infrastructure. Additionally, it would be beneficial to compare India to other developed and emerging nations in order to gain a global perspective. These comparisons would demonstrate the impact of digital adoption on communication in general and in specific situations.

Secondly, and perhaps most importantly, longitudinal studies are required immediately. Data was collected at a single point in time, which provided us with a snapshot of the situation. By conducting longitudinal studies that monitor the same individuals or groups over extended periods of time (e.g., years), researchers can observe the evolution of social media behaviours and their long-term impact on communication skills, mental health, academic performance, and social development. This would assist in the clarification of the cause-and-effect relationships, rather than merely the correlations, thereby providing a more comprehensive understanding of the impact of long-term exposure to digital technology on individuals as they mature. These types of studies may also investigate the effectiveness of digital literacy programs and the establishment of boundaries over time.

Future research should investigate specific methodologies in order to acquire these more profound and extensive insights. Neuroimaging research, such as functional magnetic resonance imaging (fMRI), could provide us with objective information regarding the impact of social media use on brain activity associated with attention, empathy, and reward systems. Ethnographic research, which entails the close observation of individuals and communities in their natural digital and offline environments, has the potential to generate comprehensive, detailed qualitative data regarding human behaviour. Using large-scale survey panels that monitor thousands of individuals over time, researchers would be able to identify statistical changes in behaviour and generalised trends. Additionally, experimental methodologies could be employed to investigate the direct impact of specific social media features or interventions on human communication.

Collectively, these diverse methodologies would enable us to acquire a more comprehensive and accurate understanding of the interconnected contradiction. Lastly, additional research should conduct a more thorough examination of certain specific points that we have raised in our study. This encompasses an examination of the precise mechanisms by which auto-correction influences formal writing and spelling, an examination of the psychological factors that contribute to digital dependency beyond straightforward reward loops, and an assessment of the long-term efficacy of various teaching methods when they incorporate technology while maintaining fundamental communication skills. Additionally, an essential new layer to our understanding of the family ecology in the digital age would be added by examining the thoughts and behaviours of parents, rather than solely their interactions with teachers.

The Evolution of Technology: What Are the Next Steps for Humans to Connect?

Technology is perpetually evolving, introducing new platforms, services, and methods of communication. Consequently, our understanding of the manner in which individuals establish connections in the digital era must be updated on a regular basis. What is "next" in human connection is already in progress, and it presents new questions and challenges that require our consideration and resolution.

The Metaverse and other immersive digital experiences are gaining popularity, which could further obscure the lines between real and virtual presence. Consider conducting work meetings in a shared virtual office space rather than on a flat video screen. Spatial audio would create the illusion of being present, while avatars would replicate body language. Consider attending university lectures or participating in group projects in virtual environments that resemble and feel like authentic classrooms or laboratories. As our digital personas become increasingly resembling actual individuals, what will be the impact on our sense of self, our capacity to establish genuine connections, and the significance of "face-to-face" communication? Will the distinctions between our online and offline identities become even more ambiguous? What psychological effects does the prolonged immersion in these fabricated environments have on us?

In the same vein, advancements in conversational AI and AI companions are transforming digital entities that are capable of conversing with humans into entities that are increasingly resembling humans. Artificial intelligence is increasingly influencing our daily communication. There are chatbots that can assist us in managing our emotions, as well as virtual assistants that can learn our preferences and requirements. What does it mean to depend on these AI entities for emotional support or social connection? Will AI-powered tools facilitate communication with others, thereby enhancing our social skills, or will they reduce our reliance on direct communication, potentially resulting in a gradual decline in our social abilities as we become accustomed to conversing with algorithms that are always correct and do not judge us? The ethical concerns that arise during the development of these AI companions, particularly in terms of their potential impact on human social requirements and relationships, are of considerable significance.

The manner in which individuals utilise social media will continue to evolve as the platforms themselves evolve, introducing new features, content categories, and revenue streams. The transition to live streaming, highly personalised algorithmic feeds, and more short-lived content suggests that digital interactions will become even more intense, rapid, and potentially addictive in the future. In order to comprehend these novel patterns and their implications for human connection, it will be necessary to remain vigilant, adjust, and conduct research in order to anticipate the subsequent phase of the connected conundrum.

One final reflection: We are shaping our digital future one conversation at a time.
As we conclude this journey, one unmistakable message emerges: the future of human interaction in the digital era is not predetermined. Although technology wields considerable influence, we, as individuals and as a society, continue to have the ability to influence its impact. The connected paradox necessitates resolution; it is not a problem that must be resolved.

The broader concepts explored in this book and our research in Idukki serve as a reminder that digital tools are highly beneficial and can engage a large number of individuals. However, they cannot and should not entirely replace the profundity of face-to-face communication. The subtlety of a voice, the warmth of a shared grin, the comfort of a knowing look, and the empathy that results from being genuinely present—these are the qualities that unite us and make us human.

Therefore, the call to action is unequivocal: it is within the power of each individual to forge their own path in the digital realm. It is imperative that we cease the passive utilisation of technology and instead begin the process of actively influencing our digital existence. This implies that we must actively determine when, why, and how we employ technology, rather than allowing it to dictate our behaviour. It entails a greater awareness of our technology usage, the establishment of distinct boundaries, and the prioritisation of our health and happiness over the constant need to remain connected.

It is crucial to maintain the long-term value of authenticity through proactive engagement. In a world where online personas are meticulously selected and reality is filtered, being genuinely authentic, open, and present in our interactions becomes a potent method of resisting and establishing connections. In order to underscore the significance of genuine human connection, it is necessary to prioritise the imperfection, spontaneity, and messiness of real-life interactions over the perfection and polish of the digital highlight reel. This entails the establishment of environments in which individuals are free to be themselves without feeling compelled to perform at a high level.

Ultimately, it is imperative that we strive to establish a vision for a digital future that is equitable. In this scenario, technology will assist individuals rather than the other way around. In the future, the fundamental human desire for deep, sympathetic, and present connection is fiercely preserved and cultivated, while the benefits of digital connectivity—such as the ability to collaborate across borders, the ease of access to knowledge, and the diversity of communities—are responsibly utilised. It is imperative that individuals, educators, parents, tech corporations, and legislators continue to collaborate and engage in dialogue regarding this matter. We can all contribute to the development of a digital future in which the profound power of human connection is bolstered, not diminished, by connectivity, one meaningful conversation at a time. This can be accomplished by consciously determining the manner and timing of our technology use, prioritising genuine presence, and instructing ourselves and future generations on how to effectively utilise technology.

Conclusion: Strategies for Navigating the Connected Future

As we conclude our investigation, it is clear that the digital revolution, which was facilitated by the pervasive adoption of social media, has significantly altered the manner in which individuals communicate with one another. Our journey has brought us to a profound "connected paradox": a world in which we are more connected than ever before, yet we are simultaneously grappling with the gradual loss of our most fundamental form of communication—face-to-face interaction—as a result of the unique experiences of students and teachers in Idukki.

Our research has provided us with critical real-world evidence that there is a robust, albeit intricate, correlation between the use of social media and in-person communication. It is not as straightforward as substituting one item with another. Rather, it is a complex ballet in which digital platforms influence the frequency, quality, and occasionally the effectiveness of our communication. We have observed how social media can facilitate learning and provide support when things go awry by uniting individuals and fostering collaboration. However, we have also observed its negative aspects: the stress associated with meticulously curated online personas, the subtle allure of distraction, the privacy risks, and the evident impact on fundamental skills such as formal writing and critical thinking, as observed by the same educators who are instructing the next generation.

The lessons from Idukki are a small illustration of a more substantial issue that necessitates a thoughtful and balanced approach. It is impossible to return to the past, and it is unwise to do so. Its benefits are incalculable, and its consequences are profound. Rather, the most critical aspect is to acquire the ability to navigate this muddled reality. This entails leveraging the remarkable opportunities that social media presents to collaborate, learn, and connect, while simultaneously cultivating the self-control necessary to circumvent its hazards. It implores a re-dedication to digital literacy, which equips individuals with the necessary resources to critically assess information, safeguard their privacy, and engage in online interactions with empathy and responsibility.

The manner in which individuals interact with one another will continue to evolve at an unprecedented pace in the future. The distinctions between our physical and digital lives will become even more blurry as new technologies such as augmented reality, virtual reality, and potent AI are introduced. This will present novel obstacles regarding engagement, identity, and presence. Future research must monitor these changes by conducting long-term studies that examine their long-term effects and expanding the scope of studies to encompass a broader range of cultural and socio-economic settings in order to obtain a comprehensive understanding.

Ultimately, each of us possesses the ability to create our digital future. By prioritising face-to-face conversations, engaging in active listening, establishing healthy digital boundaries, and establishing environments that prioritise genuine human presence, we can ensure that the technologies we develop do not undermine our remarkable capacity for connection. The meticulous decisions we make, one conversation at a time, are the beginning and the end of the journey towards a genuinely connected future.